DVD

Confidential 2

the sequel

OSBORNE

DVD
Confidential 2
the sequel

Marc Saltzman

 OSBORNE

New York • Chicago • San Francisco
Lisbon • London • Madrid • Mexico City • Milan
New Delhi • San Juan • Seoul • Singapore • Sydney • Toronto

The McGraw·Hill Companies

McGraw-Hill/Osborne
2100 Powell Street, 10th Floor
Emeryville, California 94608
U.S.A.

To arrange bulk purchase discounts for sales promotions, premiums, or fund-raisers, please contact **McGraw-Hill**/Osborne at the above address. For information on translations or book distributors outside the U.S.A., please see the International Contact Information page at the end of this book.

DVD Confidential 2: The Sequel

1234567890 DOC DOC 019876543

ISBN 0-07-222986-1

Publisher Brandon A. Nordin	**Proofreader** Pamela Vevea
Vice President & Associate Publisher Scott Rogers	**Composition** Lucie Ericksen
Acquisitions Editor Marjorie McAneny	**Illustrators** Lyssa Wald Melinda Moore Lytle Kathleen Fay Edwards
Project Editor Madhu Prasher	
Acquisitions Coordinator Tana Allen	**Series Design** Lucie Ericksen Lyssa Wald Peter F. Hancik
Copy Editor Kathy Krause	**Cover Design** Jeff Weeks

This book was composed with Corel VENTURA™ Publisher.

Dedication

This book is dedicated to Kellie: my wife, best friend, and favorite person in the world to watch DVDs with! This book is also dedicated to my delicious one-year-old twins Jacob and Maya.

About the Author

Marc Saltzman has reported on the high-tech industry for the past seven years as a freelance journalist, author, lecturer, consultant, and radio and TV personality. His specialties lie in video gaming, gadgets, DVDs, computer software and hardware, the Internet and consumer electronics. One of the first journalists in the world to break open the MP3 phenomenon in late 1997 on CNN.com, Saltzman correctly predicted this controversial audio file format would revolutionize the recording industry.

Along with his weekly syndicated columns with Gannett News Service, USAToday.com, and CNN.com, Saltzman contributes to over three dozen prominent publications, including *USA Today, Newsweek, The Los Angeles Times, Modern Maturity, Playboy*/Playboy.com, *National Post, Tribute* magazine, and many more. Saltzman has written ten books and produced two CDs, he hosts multiple radio and TV shows in Canada, and he serves as a regular on-air technology expert to CNN and CNN Headline News.

Saltzman lives in Richmond Hill, Ontario, Canada, with his wife and two children.

Table of Contents

Acknowledgments

A very special thank you goes out to the movie studios—namely Fox, Universal, DreamWorks, Disney/Buena Vista, Paramount, Columbia TriStar, Warner Bros., New Line Cinema, MGM, Artisan, Lions Gate, HBO, Miramax, USA Entertainment, Anchor Bay Entertainment, LucasFilm, and Image Entertainment—who so graciously supplied us with all the materials and information we needed to put this exciting book together. Also, thank you to the wonderful acquisitions editor Margie McAneny for her sage guidance and encouragement—and a hearty congratulations on the new addition to her family. I'd also like to thank the following folks at McGraw-Hill/Osborne—you wouldn't have this special book in your hands without their tireless work and savoir-faire: editor extraordinaire Madhu Prasher, affable publisher Roger Stewart, acquisitions coordinator Tana Allen, copy editor Kathy Krause, designers Lyssa Wald and Peter Hancik, illustrators Melinda Lytle and Kathleen Edwards, art director Jeff Weeks, and marketing manager Kate Viotto. Many special thanks to Lucie Ericksen for her skillful composition and book design. I'd also like to thank Marc Edward Heuck, "Movie Geek," for his foreword to the book.

Foreword

I didn't want to like DVD.

I had been a staunch laserdisc proponent since 1989, when I bought some unopened discs at a science fiction convention without even owning a player. Over the years, I ultimately bought three players, all second-hand, along with over 100 discs. I touted their impressive sound and proper matteing of widescreen movies to whoever would listen, and found myself often making VHS dubs of the better discs. (And I mastered the art of disguising side breaks on tape in the process too—almost seamless!)

Then came DVD, with its compact size and virtual duplication of all the features I had loved about laser. I was terrified. I had lived through the abandonment of Beta, 8-track, and the RCA CED disc format, not to mention the failure of the "digital compact cassette," and I was not about to replace my technology again. Besides, while DVD then was a new releases/blockbuster hit-driven medium, laser had reached a point where the great obscure films were finally getting released. I feared that it would easily take ten years for those kinds of films to get released in DVD, and that would depend on whether the format lasted that long. I gleefully searched magazines and web sites for flaws, and sure enough, those early DVDs did possess compression problems, lockups, awkward side breaks, and other manner of imperfections that I tried to scare potential buyers with.

Well, we all know who won this one, don't we? The technology improved, along with the presentations, and the added value elements that I loved of laser—trailers, stills, documentaries—multiplied exponentially. And while there are still a staggering number of titles unavailable as of press time, I am amazed and gratified at the number of rarities that have been pressed onto those lil' silver platters. I still do not own as many DVDs as laserdiscs, but I'll be there soon enough. (I have kept all my lasers too, because the small problem that will always plague DVD is that certain laserdiscs I love and cherish will never be able to be duplicated in this format, thanks to rights lapses and lawyers. So if you got that set of Criterion James Bond titles with the Terence Young commentaries and the Wonder Bread ads, don't you dare sell them. They ain't coming back—ever.)

The subject of this book you're holding—the DVD Easter egg—I've often found myself having to defend to the uninitiated. Not all people possess a sense of adventure, and that often applies not only to the movies they watch, but also to how they watch them. "Huh? Widescreen composition? 5.1 vs. 2.0 sound? Languages, subtitles? Please, just fill my entire TV screen and make sure it's in English—is it too late to go back to VHS?" (And sadly, there are many craven individuals in the industry who will cater to that indifference.) So it is with the Easter egg. Even the cinephile often moans that they aren't interested in a hunting expedition when they watch DVD; if this feature is so funny, then announce it on the cover so I can find it easily. But that negates the whole joke. While some eggs are long and involved, such as the *Wizard of Oz*–themed *Rocky Horror Picture Show* option, some eggs seem somewhat superfluous; a clip of Udo Kier irritating the sound man on the *Suspiria* disc is hardly a selling point, but for those of us who love the movie, it's fun.

The Easter egg symbolizes the reward to the hardcore film fan like myself, the person who held out for the best quality presentation, and access to as many ancillary items about the film that can be had. When we love a film, we often want as much as we can on it, just like the Aerosmith fan who must own every magazine cover or alternate single mix. The Easter egg is that piece of ephemera that means nothing to the layman, but brings a smile to our face. And seeing as how before DVD, we often spent time hunting through video stores and "gray-market" dealers for the preferred version of our movies (enduring fifth generation bootlegs of *The Beyond*, frantically looking for first-issue tapes of *Slap Shot* before the reissued "music changed for home video" editions), the Easter egg is a fond reminder of those days. A safe way to look for more from that favorite film.

Granted, this book is simplifying the search for you. You won't have to press buttons at random to find the eggs anymore as I did before this book was written. But if you're like me, you spent enough time on the fruitless hunt. For once, it's nice to have a map to the treasure. Enjoy the spoils, we've earned them!

Marc Edward Heuck

Introduction

We knew we had a hit on our hands with the quirky *DVD Confidential: Hundreds of Hidden Easter Eggs Revealed!*—the first book of its kind that not only celebrated this interactive medium known as the DVD but also revealed these fun secrets tucked away on hundreds of today's discs—but we didn't anticipate *how* successful it would be. In fact, thanks to strong word-of-mouth buzz among film fans (the same way Easter egg secrets are spread!), *DVD Confidential: Hundreds of Hidden Easter Eggs Revealed!* saw its fourth printing in as many months, thus becoming a "must have" stocking stuffer during last year's holiday season.

Now what does a savvy movie studio do when they've created a hit flick? Work on a well-timed sequel, of course. And this book is no exception! But what you're holding in your hands is hardly a shameless attempt to cash in on a craze—*DVD Confidential 2: The Sequel* is really two books in one. It features all 300+ Easter eggs from the first book, while adding more than 350 new Easter eggs on current and classic titles.

What's that? Never heard of Easter eggs until now? Didn't snag the first book? No worries. Let's take a step back before we continue...

Easter eggs are hidden surprises on many of today's DVD movies and TV show box sets—most of which are revealed by punching in the correct combination of buttons on the DVD remote. The Easter egg can be any number of fun extras: a blooper reel, deleted scenes, alternate endings, hidden trailers, musical scores or videos, cartoons, interviews, video games, a personal message from the director or stars, and so forth.

Remember, we're not referring to the extra features listed on the back of the DVD box; these concealed gems reward those savvy and determined enough to find them. They're inserted at the request of the filmmaker or planted by the creators of the disc itself.

So, if they're such a secret, how do you find out about them?

You're holding it.

DVD Confidential 2: The Sequel—just like *DVD Confidential: Hundreds of Hidden Easter Eggs Revealed*! before it—is your one-stop guide to the very finest in DVD Easter eggs.

Inside this book, you'll find countless eggs for DVD movies you may have in your collection, and of course, instructions for how to unlock them and what the payoff is. So be forewarned—consider this book the ultimate spoiler!

Keep in mind that some Easter eggs are easier to find than others, but we've decided to include a few of these not-so-hidden ones, too. If the goodies aren't listed on the back of the box, they're still considered "eggs"—and will be an added bonus for those buying or renting the flick.

So whether you're a hardcore film fanatic, casual movie watcher, or somewhere in between, be sure to grab some popcorn, put your feet up, and turn the page to discover more than 700 eggs tucked away inside the best of today's and yesterday's DVDs!

The question remains: Will you keep these secrets?

The Adventures of Buckaroo Banzai: Across the 8th Dimension

MGM ★ Released 1984 **★ Directed by** W.D. Richter **★ Starring** Peter Weller, John Lithgow, Ellen Barkin, Christopher Lloyd, Jeff Goldblum

Don't you hate it when you devise a machine to enter the Eighth Dimension but then an evil army of aliens comes through the portal to take over the Earth? That's basically the premise of this fun sci-fi adventure.

As a treat for fans of the film, there are a few good eggs on this disc. From the main menu, press the Left Arrow and the middle car at the top of the screen will turn green. Press Enter to read ten famous quotes from the film, such as, "No matter where you go, there you are"— B. Banzai.

The second egg can also be found from the main menu. Press the Left Arrow twice and the yellow dot in the top left-hand corner of the screen will turn green. Press Enter to scroll some alternative DVD menu designs. There are more than 35 of them in all!

Now go back to the main menu and scroll down to "Special Features." Select the "Deleted Scenes Archives" option. Once inside, scroll down four times to highlight the words "Special Features" at the bottom of the screen—but don't press Enter just yet. Instead, tap the Left Arrow and a watermelon in the lower left-hand corner of the screen will be highlighted. Press Enter to read an amusing story entitled "Food from the Skies?" from the fictitious *New Jersey Times*.

On the second page of this fake newspaper article, press the Up Arrow and the Buckaroo Banzai logo will turn green. Press Enter to watch an interview snippet with the director about the watermelon scene! He'll be handed a watermelon during the clip, too. Cute.

But wait, there's more!

Go back to the "Special Features" page and click on "More" to go to the second page. The last option is "Banzai Institute Archives." Select it. Once inside, scroll all the way to the bottom to highlight the words "Special Features" and tap the Right Arrow. A Buckaroo Banzai logo will now be circled in green. Press Enter to access a couple of alternative DVD box designs for this movie.

The Adventures of Priscilla, Queen of the Desert

MGM ★ **Released** 1994 ★ **Directed by** Stephan Elliott ★ **Starring** Terence Stamp, Hugo Weaving, Guy Pearce, Bill Hunter

In this hilarious comedy, three drag queens get a cabaret gig—in the middle of the Australian desert! Talk about a sizzling show....

And of course this DVD has a little something extra to find. From the main menu, simply press the Up Arrow once on the DVD remote and a pink star will appear in the center of the screen. Press Enter to access a hidden section, entitled "Life's a Drag," that examines the history of drag queens and female impersonators from the 1820s up to the 1990s. Great fun!

Alien

20th Century Fox ★ **Released** 1979 ★ **Directed by** Ridley Scott ★ **Starring** Tom Skerritt, Sigourney Weaver, Veronica Cartwright, Harry Dean Stanton, John Hurt, Ian Holm, Yaphet Kotto

Alien is the first adventure in one of the most beloved sci-fi film series in history. The story begins as the crew of the spaceship *Nostromo* investigates a transmission from an "uninhabited" planet. However, something gets back on the ship with them and begins to attack crew members one by one. It's definitely one of those DVDs to watch with the lights off and the speakers cranked.

To access the eggs on this DVD (also found in the Alien Legacy Box Set), pop in the disc, and from the main menu, scroll down once and select "Extra Features." Once inside, scroll down to the bottom, and the acid pool on the floor will turn red. Press Enter to peruse a handful of interactive screens that outline the four stages of the alien's life cycle: "egg," "facehugger," "chestburster," and then "adult."

Now go back to the main menu, and highlight the words "Extra Features"—but don't press Enter just yet. Instead, tap the Left Arrow on the DVD remote, and the picture on the left side of the screen will now have a white border. Press Enter and the "camera" will swivel around to display the hidden credits for the making of this DVD.

Lastly, from the main menu again, highlight the words "Scene Selection," but don't hit Enter just yet. Press the Right Arrow, and the picture on the right of the screen will illuminate. Press Enter to view the *Nostromo* flight plan and some detailed (but of course, fictitious) information about each of the crew members. There are roughly four pages of dossier info and images for each of the seven crew members.

Great stuff!

Aliens: Special Edition

20th Century Fox ★ Released 1986 ★ **Directed by** James Cameron ★ **Starring** Sigourney Weaver

The terror continues as Lt. Ellen Ripley (Sigourney Weaver)—the sole survivor from the last alien encounter—joins a crew of space marines to look into the disappearance of colonists on LV-426.

This "Special Edition" DVD (also found in the Alien Legacy Box Set) features a couple of hidden surprises.

Pop in the disc and from the main menu, enter the "Extra Features" section. Once inside, scroll down to "Theatrical Trailers" to watch all the theatrical trailers to all four *Alien* films. These are not documented on the back of the DVD box.

Also, here's a small egg: While still in the "Extra Features" screen, scroll down five times until the vital signs display at the bottom of the screen has an orange border. Now press Enter to view the credits for the making of this disc.

Alien³

20th Century Fox ★ **Released** 1992 ★ **Directed by** David Fincher ★
Starring Sigourney Weaver

Immediately following the events of *Aliens,* the spaceship carrying home Lieutenant Ripley (Sigourney Weaver) and other space marines home crash lands on a prison planet. Ripley is left alone (without any weapons) to deal with the cause of the crash—a stowaway alien. As if this weren't stressful enough, Ripley soon discovers another horrifying truth about this beast's intentions.

From the main menu of this DVD, scroll up and enter the "Extra Features" submenu. Once inside, press Enter to select "The Making of *Alien³* Featurette." Once this lengthy documentary is over, don't turn off the player just yet. A hidden *Alien³* trailer will begin—one that features scenes from the film that ended up on the cutting room floor!

Alien Resurrection

20th Century Fox ★ **Released** 1997 ★ **Directed by** Jean-Pierre Jeunet ★
Starring Sigourney Weaver, Winona Ryder

You'd think Lieutenant Ripley (Sigourney Weaver) would choose another career path after three deadly alien encounters, yet she's back again. OK, to be fair, it's a cloned version of Ripley who was created to combat the creatures 200 years after the first three *Alien* adventures. She is joined by Annalee Call (Winona Ryder), a mechanic with a few surprises of her own.

Just as with the "Special Edition" *Aliens* DVD, undocumented theatrical trailers to all four *Alien* movies are planted on this disc.

Pop in the DVD, and from the main menu, select the "Extra Features" section. Along with the lengthy featurette on the making of this movie, you'll notice original theatrical trailers for *Alien, Aliens, Alien³,* and *Alien Resurrection.*

Top 10 Reasons Why DVDs Are Better than VHS

Let's face it—your bulky videocassettes are so 20th century. Other than the fact that *most* DVDs are not recordable (yet), they're far superior to videocassettes.

How are DVDs better than videotape? Let us count the ways:

1. Video—More than double the resolution of VHS.
2. Audio—Forget stereo speakers, we're talking 5.1 surround sound or greater.
3. Size—DVDs take up much less space.
4. Capacity—DVDs hold much more data than VHS tapes (i.e., extra features).
5. Cueing—No waiting to fast-forward or rewind tapes (remember that?).
6. Durability—DVDs last longer and have fewer parts to break.
7. Versatility—The same DVDs for your TV also work on computers with DVD-ROM drives.
8. Captions—Thanks to the optional subtitles, DVDs are great for those with impaired hearing.
9. Languages—Want to watch a movie in your mother tongue? Many DVDs offer alternate language tracks.
10. Extras—Easter eggs!

Almost Famous—Untitled: The Bootleg Cut

DreamWorks Pictures ★ **Released** 2000 ★ **Directed by** Cameron Crowe ★ **Starring** Patrick Fugit, Billy Crudup, Jason Lee, Kate Hudson, Frances McDormand, Anna Paquin, Philip Seymour Hoffman, Fairuza Balk, Noah Taylor

In this somewhat autobiographical tale penned and directed by Cameron Crowe, a 15-year-old boy goes on tour with a rock band and writes about his adventures for *Rolling Stone* magazine.

This "Bootleg Cut" double DVD features a few good eggs, too.

Insert the first disc, and from the main menu, scroll across and highlight the words "Special Features." Once inside this new menu screen, tap the Right Arrow on the DVD remote to highlight the words "Love Comes and Goes"—but don't press Enter just yet. Instead, tap the Up Arrow and the Polaroid picture on the right will turn red. Press Enter to watch an amusing outtake with Kate Hudson trying to get the name "Leslie" right, preceded by a lengthy explanation by Crowe.

Now go back to the main menu and select "Audio." Click over to the words "Commentary by Director Cameron Crowe," and then press the Right Arrow. The hole in the middle of the record will turn red; press Enter to be treated to an eerie outtake with actors Philip Seymour Hoffman and Patrick Fugit—but pay close attention to Crowe's explanation before the clip begins.

There's also a secret Easter egg on the second DVD: Pop in the disc, and from the main menu, select "Special Features." Now click on the "Cast" section, and once inside, choose the biography of Fairuza "Sapphire" Balk. Now press the Up Arrow, and the middle Polaroid picture of her will turn red. Press Enter to hear Crowe chat about working on this film, followed by an outtake of a deleted scene on the tour bus.

American Pie: Collector's Edition

Universal Pictures ★ Released 1999 ★ **Directed by** Paul Weitz ★
Starring Jason Biggs, Chris Klein, Natasha Lyonne, Thomas Ian Nicholas, Tara Reid, Mena Suvari, Shannon Elizabeth, Alyson Hannigan, Seann William Scott, Eddie Kaye Thomas, Eugene Levy

This critically acclaimed comedy looks at the lives of four teenage boys who make a pact to lose their virginity by prom night. As expected, things don't go exactly as planned— for better or for worse.

From the main menu, select "Bonus Materials" and then enter the second page of these special features. Now click on "Recommendations" to watch three full, undocumented trailers to *Animal House, American Graffiti,* and *The Blues Brothers.* What a treat!

Here's another one—sit through the commercial for the *American Pie* soundtrack, and then enjoy the music video to Tonic's "You Wanted More," which should start immediately afterward.

These eggs do not exist on the "Ultimate Edition" of *American Pie.*

What You May Not Know About Vertigo

For the purposes of shooting *Vertigo* (page 174), Hitchcock developed the famous simultaneous use of forward zoom and reverse tracking shot—used in hundreds of movies today. This was used in *Vertigo* to convey the illness when James Stewart's character was looking down a flight of winding stairs in the tower.

American Pie 2: Collector's Edition

Universal Pictures ★ **Released** 2001 ★ **Directed by** James B. Rogers ★
Starring Jason Biggs, Shannon Elizabeth, Alyson Hannigan, Chris Klein,
Natasha Lyonne, Thomas Ian Nicholas, Tara Reid, Seann William Scott,
Mena Suvari, Eddie Kaye Thomas, Eugene Levy

They're back! In this sequel to the hit comedy of '99, the gang has returned from a year away at college for an all-new summer adventure.

This "Collector's Edition" DVD features more than ten hours of extra features and a real Easter egg surprise.

From the main menu, select "Bonus Materials" and then enter the second page by clicking on the small arrow at the bottom of the screen. Now, instead of selecting one of these options, push the Up Arrow on the remote, and the words "Bonus Materials" will illuminate in red. Press Enter and let cast members Jason Biggs, Thomas Ian Nicholas, and Mena Suvari treat you to what you're after. You've been warned....

An American Werewolf in London: Collector's Edition

Universal Studios ★ **Released** 1981 ★ **Directed by** John Landis ★ **Starring** David Naughton, Jenny Agutter, Griffin Dunne

This modern cult classic straddles horror and dark comedy, when two American students head to Europe on a backpacking expedition. Thanks to a vicious werewolf attack, one student ends up dead, and the other is hospitalized and suffers from monstrous nightmares.

Fans of the film can find a hidden trailer on this "Collector's Edition" DVD—if you know where to look, that is.

From the main menu, scroll up and press Enter over the words "Bonus Materials." Then select the word "Recommendations" on the lower right of the screen. On the second page is an image of the DVD for the classic film *The Wolf Man*. If you take a closer look, you'll notice a small video reel underneath it. Press the Up Arrow on the remote, and the reel will turn white. Now press Enter to watch a rare trailer for the timeless black-and-white film.

An Evening with Kevin Smith

New Wave Entertainment/Columbia TriStar Home Entertainment ★
Released 2002 ★ **Directed by** J.M. Kenny ★ **Starring** Kevin Smith

Silent Bob speaks! Writer/director/actor Kevin Smith engages in hilarious Q&A discussions with college students from around the country.

Believe it or not, there are a whopping nine eggs on this two-disc set. Ready Freddy? Here we go....

On the first DVD, select "Subtitles" from the main menu. Once inside, scroll down to highlight the words "Main Menu"—but don't press Enter just yet. Instead, press the Left Arrow twice on the DVD remote and the circles on the chalkboard (where Kevin is kicking) will turn orange. Press Enter to see a funny question from a college student—and an even funnier answer from Kevin.

While still in this "Subtitles" submenu, use the DVD remote to highlight the word "English" and press the Left Arrow twice. The Os on the "Xs and Os" game board will turn orange. Press Enter for another fun, unreleased scene from "An Evening with Kevin Smith," when Kevin first makes his appearance at a show.

Go back to the main menu and highlight the word "Subtitles" again—but this time don't press Enter. Instead, press the Right Arrow once and the flowers on the chalkboard will turn orange. Now press Enter to see a very funny moment where a student admits to seeing one of Kevin's movies for free, followed by a good question!

Go back to the main menu again (dig the lounge music, huh?) and this time select the option entitled "Scene Selections." Now navigate over to Scene 3 and press the Down Arrow on the DVD remote. Kevin's glasses will illuminate. Press Enter to see Kevin answer how to best get your script read by a Hollywood director. It might not be the answer you'd expect!

Go to the second page of "Scene Selections" (Scenes 5 through 8) and highlight Scene 6 or 7 without pressing Enter. Press the Down Arrow three times until the chalk eraser illuminates in white. Press Enter for yet another clip—but this time the question is interrupted.

Now pop in the second disc. From the main menu, highlight the entry entitled "Play Movie" but don't press Enter. Instead, press the Up Arrow and the smiley face on the chalkboard will turn orange. Press Enter to see another great question— one that challenges Kevin's decision to cast Alanis Morissette as God in his cult film *Dogma*.

Next enter the "Subtitles" submenu and, once inside, highlight the word "English" but don't press Enter. Instead, press the Right Arrow twice and the heart on the chalkboard will turn orange. Press Enter to hear Kevin answer a question from a female fan about having sex in a car.

Now go back to the disc's main menu but this time choose "Scene Selections" from the list of options. Once inside, press the Down Arrow on the DVD remote twice and Kevin's right shoe will turn orange. Press Enter for another funny clip. Gee, remind me never to pee at a Kevin Smith show!

And finally, enter the "Trailers" submenu and, once inside, scroll down to highlight the words "Spider-Man" but don't press Enter. Instead, press the Right Arrow on the DVD remote once and the "E=mc2" on the chalkboard will turn orange. Press Enter to hear Kevin's answer as to what superhero he would be, and why.

DVD Factoids

Here are a few neat tidbits about DVDs:

- DVDs have a shelf life of over 100 years.
- According to Informa Media PLC (www.informa.com), DVD penetration will overtake VCR over the next decade. By the end of 2009, 464 million homes will have DVD players, compared with 435 million with VCRs.
- There is no mechanical wear and tear when you play a DVD; DVDs are read by lasers and can be played an unlimited number of times.

The Animal

Columbia Pictures ★ Released 2001 **★ Directed** by Luke Greenfield ★
Starring Rob Schneider, Colleen Haskell, John C. McGinley, Guy Torry,
Edward Asner

Following a serious car accident, Marvin Mange (Rob Schneider) finds that his body was put back together by a deranged scientist who used animal organs, giving Mange their physical abilities. Don't you hate it when that happens?

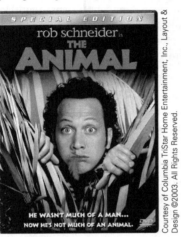

The DVD for *The Animal* features a well-hidden Easter egg. Here's how to access it: From the main menu, scroll down to select the "Special Features" section at the bottom of the screen. Once inside, go to the second page and select the feature "What's in Marvin?" Now press Enter to start the movie clip. Once it's completed, you'll be kicked out to a menu screen again, but this time there will be three pictures of animals. The lion's head will be illuminated. Press the Up Arrow twice on the DVD remote and a lion's paw will light up in the top left-hand corner of the screen. Now press Enter to enjoy a three-minute clip of deleted scenes strung together—featuring Marvin and Dr. Wilder (Michael Caton). Hilarious!

Animal Farm

Artisan ★ Released 1999 **★ Directed** by John Stephenson **★ Starring** Kelsey Grammer, Ian Holm, Julia Louis-Dreyfus, Julia Ormond, Pete Postlethwaite, Paul Scofield, Patrick Stewart, Peter Ustinov

In this made-for-TV adaptation of George Orwell's classic novel, all hell breaks loose in the peaceful Irish countryside when animals revolt against their master and take over a farm.

The DVD for the flick contains a neat little Easter egg that unlocks video footage from the film. From the main menu, select "Special Features" and then go to the section entitled "The Animal Rules." Once inside, you'll see a list of animal rules. The first set of rules is already highlighted in yellow. It says, "Whatever goes upon two legs is an enemy" and "Whatever goes upon four legs or has wings is a friend."

If you press Enter you'll see two linked video clips from the film that correspond with this set of rules.

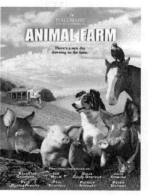

When you return to the menu, the next rule will be highlighted: "No animal shall wear clothes." Press Enter to watch this clip. Now you'll be able to select the next rule on this page: "No animal shall sleep in a bed." But after viewing this video clip, you'll now see the new words "with sheets" scribbled after the sentence. Watch the next rule—"No animal shall drink alcohol"—and when you return, it'll now include the words "to excess." The next rule says, "No animal shall kill another animal," which will then change to "…without cause." Finally, click on the last rule—"All animals are equal"—and watch the clip. When you return to the screen, it'll say, "All animals are equal, but some are more equal than others."

These changed rules and corresponding movie clips work only if you click the rules in the correct order.

Antz

DreamWorks Pictures ★ Released 1998 ★ **Directed by** Eric Darnell, Tim Johnson ★ **Starring** Woody Allen, Dan Aykroyd, Anne Bancroft, Jane Curtin, Danny Glover, Gene Hackman, Jennifer Lopez, John Mahoney, Paul Mazursky, Grant Shaud, Sylvester Stallone, Sharon Stone, Christopher Walken

In this animated adventure, Z (voice of Woody Allen) is a small ant with some big ideas—one of which is to land Princess Bala (voice of Sharon Stone) as his girlfriend. He convinces his soldier buddy Weaver (voice of Sylvester Stallone) to switch places with him to get closer to her, and his mundane life takes a wild turn.

This DVD contains a number of special features and a little-known egg, too.

From the main menu, go to the "Special Features" screen. If you look closely, you'll see a small white DreamWorks logo on the bottom leaf (along the left portion of the screen). To access it, press the Left Arrow followed by the Down Arrow, and the leaf should now be highlighted.

Press Enter to watch an enjoyable animated credits screen for this DVD of *Antz*, playing to the song "I Can See Clearly Now."

Apollo 13: Collector's Edition

Universal Studios ★ **Released** 1995 ★ **Directed by** Ron Howard ★ **Starring** Tom Hanks, Kevin Bacon, Bill Paxton, Gary Sinise, Ed Harris

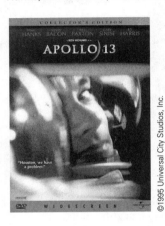

©1995 Universal City Studios, Inc.

"Houston, we have a problem."

Apollo 13 is based on a true story chronicling the ill-fated journey of a "routine space flight" to the moon in 1970. The three astronauts on board—Jim Lovell, Fred Haise, and Jack Swigert, as played by Tom Hanks, Bill Paxton, and Kevin Bacon, respectively—must come to grips with their near-impossible task of making it back home alive.

Directed by Ron Howard, *Apollo 13* was one of the more critically acclaimed and commercially successful films of 1995.

As a special—and secret—treat, the entire musical score to the film is hidden on this disc (and in Dolby Digital!).

Here's how to access it—do nothing!

Insert the DVD and let the main menu screen load, and you can now toggle between each of the classical audio tracks by pressing the right and left Skip buttons on the remote. Enjoy!

Groovy Sales, Baby—Just Groovy

The third James Bond spoof in Mike Myer's shagadelic spy series, *Austin Powers in Goldmember* (page 15) is the most successful Austin Powers installment to date, grossing more than $212 "mil-ee-un" dollars at the box office. The entire Austin Powers franchise has earned a total of $470 million at the U.S. box office. Oh behave, Austin!

Atlantis: The Lost Empire, Collector's Edition

Walt Disney Pictures ★ **Released** 2001 ★ **Directed by** Gary Trousdale, Kirk Wise ★ **Starring** Michael J. Fox

In this animated adventure set in the year 1914, Milo Thatch (voice of Michael J. Fox) is a young adventurer who joins a brave group of explorers to find the lost continent of Atlantis.

This two-disc "Collector's Edition" DVD is jam-packed with extra features including visual commentaries, a "DisneyPedia," deleted scenes, animation production featurettes, and much more.

With all that work, the team responsible for this DVD should be acknowledged, no? The Easter egg will unlock the credits screen.

Insert the second disc, dubbed "Supplemental Features," and from the main menu, select the word "Explore." Once inside, scroll down to highlight the section "Animation Production," but don't press Enter just yet. Instead, press the Right Arrow, and the words "DVD Credits" will appear. Now press Enter to read the credits on the making of this double-disc set.

Austin Powers: International Man of Mystery

New Line Cinema ★ **Released** 1997 ★ **Directed by** Jay Roach ★ **Starring** Mike Myers, Elizabeth Hurley

Oh, behave!

This groovy film stars Mike Myers as Austin Powers, a secret agent frozen in the '60s and thawed back into action in the '90s to battle his archenemy, Dr. Evil (also played by Myers). Can Powers and his sexy sidekick, Ms. Kensington (Elizabeth Hurley), manage to stop Dr. Evil's plot to control the world?

Pop in either side of the DVD ("Standard" or Widescreen"), and from the main menu, select "Extra Stuff." Now scroll down four times, select "The Cast," and then choose "Mimi Rogers." On the second page of her biography is a pink star beside the *Lost in Space* tab. Select it and press Enter to watch a lengthy trailer to the sci-fi film. On the same bio screen, look at the bottom and you'll find a video clip of Rogers in *Monkey Trouble;* there's also a third video clip of her in *The Rapture* on the last page of her biography.

While still inside the "The Cast" section, select Elizabeth Hurley and scroll through her bio to watch a scene of her in *Dangerous Ground.*

Another video clip, for the film *Wide Sargasso Sea,* can be found in Michael York's biography.

Austin Powers: The Spy Who Shagged Me

New Line Cinema ★ **Released** 1999 ★ **Directed by** Jay Roach ★ **Starring** Mike Myers, Heather Graham

Shagalicious, baby! This follow-up to the 1997 James Bond spoof (*Austin Powers: International Man of Mystery*) now shines the spotlight on Dr. Evil (Mike Myers) as he uses a time machine to go back to 1969 to drain Austin Powers (also Mike Myers) of his "mojo." Powers also heads back in time with the aid of his sexy sidekick Felicity Shagwell (Heather Graham). Dr. Evil's sidekick is a clone of himself—but about one eighth his size—known as "Mini Me" (Verne Troyer).

From the main menu—where an animated Powers dances and dishes out his oh-so-sexy lines such as "Click it—you're making me randy, baby"— select the "Special Features" option.

Don't touch anything—let Austin continue with his silly antics. After about 30 seconds, Dr. Evil's phallic spaceship will appear, soaring from the bottom of the screen up to the top, leaving behind a large *E* in the middle of the screen. Navigate to it and press Enter once the *E* turns red. The *E* will turn green. The screen will then flip to the hidden "Dr. Evil's Special Features" page, which includes four special sections: the lengthy "Comedy Central's Canned Ham: The Dr. Evil Story" (a mock documentary, or "mocumentary"!), two music video-esque excerpts from the film ("What if God Was One of Us" and "Just the Two of Us," both performed by Dr. Evil and Mini-Me), and "Classic Evil Schemes Gone Awry," a humorous look at foiled attempts at killing the protagonist in classic films.

Also, you may notice the small New Line Cinema logo underneath "Special Features." Scroll down and select this to be taken to numerous pages from companies responsible for the making of this disc.

Austin Powers in Goldmember

New Line Cinema ★ **Released** 2002 ★ **Directed by** Jay Roach ★ **Starring** Mike Myers, Beyoncé Knowles, Seth Green, Michael York, Robert Wagner, Mindy Sterling, Verne Troyer, Michael Caine

This groovy third film in the popular series pits Mini-Me (Verne Troyer), Dr. Evil (Mike Myers), and a new villain, Goldmember (also Mike Myers) against the hairy-chested international man of mystery, Austin Powers (once again, Mike Myers). The evil trio kidnaps Austin's father (Michael Caine) in the year 1975, so Austin Powers goes back in time to save him and teams up with the sexy Foxy Cleopatra (Beyoncé Knowles). Great fun!

There's a small Easter egg on the DVD for the movie. From the main menu, press the Right Arrow once and the yellow Infinifilm logo will now have a blue star on it. Press Enter to read nine pages on the making of this disc, with credits for added-value materials, DVD production services, interactive menu design, pop-up prompt design, digital mastering, and more.

Also be sure to check out this DVD's shagadelic extra features.

The Best Movie Sequels

We all know most movie sequels don't match the charm of their predecessors. The following dozen films are exceptions to the rule (not listed in any particular order):

1. The Godfather: Part II
2. Star Wars: Episode V—The Empire Strikes Back
3. Aliens
4. Toy Story 2
5. The Road Warrior (Mad Max 2)
6. The Bride of Frankenstein
7. The Lord of the Rings: The Two Towers
8. American Pie 2
9. From Russia with Love
10. Terminator 2
11. Austin Powers: The Spy Who Shagged Me
12. Indiana Jones and the Last Crusade

The Avengers

Warner Bros. ★ **Released** 1998 ★ **Directed by** Jeremiah S. Chechik ★ **Starring** Ralph Fiennes, Uma Thurman, Sean Connery, Jim Broadbent

Based on the hip '60s TV series, this action-packed film stars Ralph Fiennes and Uma Thurman as two secret agents—a dapper John Steed and a sexy Emma Peel—pitted against the evil genius Sir August De Wynter (Sean Connery) and his weather-controlling machine.

Wanna see a handful of undocumented movie trailers? Pop in the disc and from the main menu scroll down and select the section entitled "Reel Recommendations." Press Enter over the words "Movie Projector," and inside you'll find a bunch of theatrical trailers to these films: *Batman & Robin* (1997), *Dangerous Liaisons* (1988), *The Man Who Would Be King* (1975), *National Lampoon's Christmas Vacation* (1989), and *U.S. Marshals* (1998).

Barbershop

MGM ★ **Released** 2002 ★ **Directed** by Tim Story ★ **Starring** Ice Cube, Anthony Anderson, Sean Patrick Thomas, Eve, Troy Garity, Michael Ealy, Leonard Earl Howze, Keith David, Cedric the Entertainer

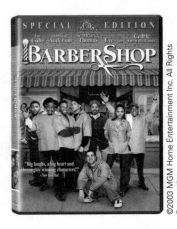

©2003 MGM Home Entertainment Inc. All Rights Reserved.

An inner-city Chicago barbershop serves as the backdrop for this surprise box-office-hit comedy starring rapper-turned-actor Ice Cube as an entrepreneur who wants to do the right thing.

The DVD for *Barbershop* includes a hairnet full of extra features such as four behind-the-scenes featurettes, an interactive game, deleted scenes with commentary, bloopers and outtakes, and more.

And, of course, there's a fun Easter egg, too. Pop in the DVD, and from the main menu select "Special Features" in the middle of the screen. Now scroll down to the word "More" but don't press Enter just yet. Instead, press the Up Arrow on the remote and the barbershop pole will illuminate. Now press Enter to be treated to a hidden feature entitled "Barber Banter," a lengthy clip of humorous interviews with real barbers who reveal what they hear from customers—be it rumors, gossip, or conspiracy theories.

Hilarious!

Basic Instinct: Special Edition

Artisan Entertainment ★ Released 1992 **★ Directed by** Paul Verhoeven ★
Starring Michael Douglas, Sharon Stone

Courtesy of Artisan Home Entertainment Inc.

Detective Nick Curran (Michael Douglas) begins investigating the kinky murder of a rock star and discovers he was killed in the same fashion as described in a novel by the deceased musician's seductive girlfriend, Catherine Tramell (Sharon Stone). This modern-day whodunit introduces new plot twists throughout the film, and thus, keeps the audience guessing on the killer's identity.

Artisan's "Special Edition" of this DVD features a few eggs—and a promotional ice-pick pen, as well!

Scroll down and select the "Special Features" section. Press the Right Arrow once to illuminate the ice pick. Press Enter and the ice pick will turn red. Now viewers can watch a lengthy rehearsal sequence with Sharon Stone—including the infamous interrogation and lie detector scenes, and two others.

Now enter the "Setup" area of the DVD, press the Right Arrow on the remote three times, and the ice pick will turn yellow. Press Enter to view more rehearsal footage—this time from Jeanne Tripplehorn, who plays Dr. Elisabeth Garner in the film.

Lastly, select the JVC logo on the bottom left of the "Setup" screen (turning it from red to yellow), and then press Enter to watch a commercial for JVC products.

Barbershop Backlash

Some members of the African American community—including civil rights pioneer Rosa Parks—were outraged at the remarks made about Parks and other black leaders in the film *Barbershop*. In fact, Parks shunned the 2003 NAACP Image Awards because the comedy had five nominations (including Best Picture) and was hosted by Cedric the Entertainer, who played the character who made the upsetting remarks in the film.

Battlefield Earth

Warner Bros. ★ **Released** 2000 ★ **Directed by** Roger Christian ★ **Starring** John Travolta, Barry Pepper, Forest Whitaker

In the year 3000, Earth is under attack from an alien race known as the Psychlos, led by the vicious alien security chief, Terl (John Travolta). Humans, of course, won't take this attempt at global domination lying down, so a rebel group lead by Jonnie Goodboy Tyler (Barry Pepper) prepares to fight back.

From the DVD's main menu, head to the section "Special Features." Once inside, tap the Right Arrow on the DVD remote, and a blue symbol will appear over the deadly machine in the picture. Press Enter to watch some never-before-released makeup work done on the actors.

While back in the "Special Features" page, click "Continue" to enter the second page of bonus materials. Now press the Right Arrow, and that same blue symbol will appear over the pyramid. Press Enter for more behind-the-scenes footage of a group of actors running through the town.

Head back to the second page of "Special Features," and choose the last option: "Cast & Crew." Try the same thing again by pressing the Right Arrow, and the blue symbol will appear over the image. Press Enter to watch some rehearsal stunt work.

Now go back to the main menu and enter the "Languages" submenu. Press the Right Arrow to watch even more stunt rehearsals.

The Beach

20th Century Fox ★ **Released** 2000 ★ **Directed by** Danny Boyle ★ **Starring** Leonardo DiCaprio, Tilda Swinton, Virginie Ledoyen, Guillaume Canet, Robert Carlyle

The adventurous Richard (Leonardo DiCaprio) is an American backpacker who travels alone to Thailand and convinces a young French couple to join him on a journey to find an island paradise.

The DVD features audio commentary by the film's director, nine deleted scenes, a storyboard gallery, a music video, and an undocumented Easter egg.

From the main menu, scroll across three times and select the word "Features." Once inside, scroll down and press Enter over the "Cast & Crew" option.

Now select the page for actor Robert Carlyle, and if you press the Left Arrow while reading his biography, his picture on the left side of the screen will illuminate in red. Press Enter to watch the full trailer for *The Full Monty*, which also stars Carlyle.

The Beastmaster

Anchor Bay Entertainment ★ **Released** 1982 ★ **Directed by** Don Coscarelli ★ **Starring** Marc Singer, Tanya Roberts, Rip Torn, John Amos

Don Coscarelli's *The Beastmaster* is a fantasy cult classic about a warrior, Dar (Marc Singer), on a journey to avenge his parents' murder. He is helped by a skilled hunter, Seth (John Amos); a beautiful slave girl, Kiri (Tanya Roberts); and the cunning ability to communicate with animals. Veteran actor Rip Torn plays the malevolent priest Maax—the one responsible for the slaughter of Dar's family.

Select "Extras" from the main menu, and you'll notice new areas to explore, such as behind-the-scenes footage, product art, posters, and still galleries. Instead of choosing one of these options, press the Right Arrow a few times to scroll down the list of options. After "Main Menu," a yellow circle will appear.

Press Enter and the circle will turn into an eye and will then cut to unreleased footage including five minutes of alternate love scenes between Dar and Kiri (with partial nudity), and in the company of a restless black tiger.

Blade II: On PCs and on Tape

Fans of this dark vampire-hunting thriller (page 24) may not have thought to pop the DVD into a computer's DVD-ROM drive. Well, you should—there are a handful of extra features only viewable on a PC. These include a script-to-screen comparison and the original web site (archived on the DVD). And as a special treat for those who own the VHS version of *Blade II*, there's a bonus Cypress Hill/Roni Size "Child of the Wild West" music video from Immortal Records.

The Beatles: Yellow Submarine

MGM ★ Released 1968 ★ **Directed by** George Dunning ★ **Starring** John Lennon, Paul McCartney, George Harrison, Ringo Starr

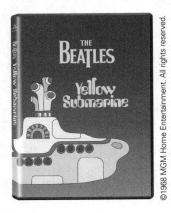

This visionary cartoon tells the tale of the Fab Four as they set sail and search for the music-hating Blue Meanies, so they can put an end to the Meanies' evil reign over the citizens of Pepperland.

The soundtrack features many of The Beatles' beloved songs, including "All You Need Is Love," "Sgt. Pepper's Lonely Hearts Club Band," and, of course, "Yellow Submarine."

A movie as surreal as this was made for hidden eggs, and thankfully, there are a number of them on the DVD.

From the disc's main menu, press the Up Arrow, and George Harrison looking out of the porthole will turn purple. Press Enter to hear an audio clip from him in the movie. The same can be done by navigating with the Right Arrow and Left Arrow buttons to select other members of the band.

You can also highlight in purple four empty portholes by moving over them using the remote. Press Enter to hear music clips and to view cartoon characters and animation.

Try moving the remote over other areas around and on the submarine, and you'll find 14 eggs.

A Beautiful Mind

Universal Pictures ★ Released 2001 ★ **Directed by** Ron Howard ★ **Starring** Russell Crowe, Ed Harris, Jennifer Connelly, Paul Bettany, Adam Goldberg, Judd Hirsch, Josh Lucas, Anthony Rapp, Christopher Plummer

This Oscar-winning tale (it won, among other things, Best Picture at the 2002 Academy Awards) lets us into the mind of a disturbed but brilliant schizophrenic, John Nash (Russell Crowe) and tells the story of how he overcame his illness (and gift) to win a Nobel Prize. The film is based on a true story.

There are a few hidden gems on this disc. From the main menu, select "Bonus Materials." Now select "More" and then choose "Now Showing" (second from the bottom). After the video montage, there are a number of hidden theatrical trailers to access, including *Apollo 13*, *The Family Man*, *K-Pax,* and *Patch Adams*.

But there's more—though selecting the film reel will launch the trailer, choosing the "Sneak Peek" option for each film will start either an interview snippet with the film's star or behind-the-scenes footage!

Bedazzled: Special Edition

20th Century Fox ★ **Released** 2000 ★ **Directed by** Harold Ramis ★ **Starring** Brendan Fraser, Elizabeth Hurley

It's hard to find a "hotter" devil than Elizabeth Hurley in this entertaining remake about a hapless computer technician, Elliot Richards (Brendan Fraser), who falls for the Princess of Darkness' seductive ways. Richards agrees to sell his soul for seven wishes, and naturally, a few unexpected strings are attached.

If you want to see one of Richards' wishes that didn't make it to the final version of the film, you'll need to unlock the Easter egg on this devilish comedy.

Pop in the DVD, and from the main menu, go to the "Special Features" area, and then select "More'" to enter the second page.

Press the Right Arrow and a little red devil will appear on the devil's left shoulder. Press Enter and sit back to watch a risqué ten-minute deleted scene in which Richards becomes a drug-addicted rock star. (Note: Due to its mature content, this segment is not for kids.)

Behind Enemy Lines

20th Century Fox ★ Released 2001 **★ Directed by** John Moore **★ Starring** Gene Hackman, Owen Wilson

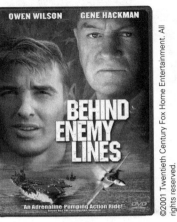

U.S. Navy pilot Chris Burnett (Owen Wilson) is shot down during a recon mission over Bosnia and must fight to stay alive until his commanding officer Leslie Reigart (Gene Hackman) can launch a renegade rescue mission—against strict NATO orders.

Allegedly, *Behind Enemy Lines* is the first film to feature the U.S. Navy's new F/A-18E/F Super Hornet.

From the main menu of this DVD, scroll down and select the "Special Features" section, and then choose the "Pre-Vis Ejection Sequence."

Now press the Up Arrow on the remote, and a red star will appear on the screen. Press Enter to watch a hidden (and humorous) outtake with actor Wilson on the back of a pickup truck.

Being John Malkovich

USA Films/Universal Pictures ★ Released 1999 **★ Directed by** Spike Jonze **★ Starring** John Cusack, Cameron Diaz, Catherine Keener, Orson Bean, Mary Kay Place, John Malkovich

In this refreshingly unique film, Craig Schwartz (John Cusack) is a struggling street puppeteer who decides to take a job as a filing clerk to make more money. He soon discovers a secret door, which serves as a portal into the brain of actor John Malkovich (played in the film by John Malkovich). Strange, but highly entertaining.

The eggs on this DVD aren't as strange as the film—nor are they too hard to find—but they're rewarding nonetheless.

On the DVD, enter the "Language Selection" section from the main menu and then don't press anything. Instead, turn up the volume, and listen to an entire song by Björk, entitled "Amphibian."

More soundtrack music from the film can be heard throughout these menu screens, such as the instrumental track on the "Special Features" page.

Now go to the second page of the "Special Features" section, and one of the choices will be "Don't enter here, there is nothing here." If you're curious, press Enter over these words to be taken to a new screen that says "There is nothing here, press enter to return."

Well, what did you expect?

Big Trouble in Little China

20th Century Fox ★ Released 1986 **★ Directed by** John Carpenter **★ Starring** Kurt Russell, Kim Cattrall

This supernatural action flick stars an unlikely hero—truck driver Jack Burton (Kurt Russell) —as he helps save his friend's fiancée, Gracie Law (Kim Cattrall), from an evil Chinatown sorcerer. Of course, he's also out to rescue his beloved truck!

Insert the second DVD and from the main menu, select the word "More," which takes you to the second page of bonus materials. Once here, scroll over to "Cast & Crew" and press Enter. Now press the Left Arrow, and you'll notice a yellow outline surrounding actor James Hong. Press Enter to read his filmography. Keep pressing the Right Arrow to access the filmography for the other cast and crew members.

Now go to the third page of "Special Features" (by pressing "More" again), and scroll down to highlight the words "Richard Edlund Interview." Instead of pressing Enter, tap the Right Arrow and a pair of yellow eyes will appear on the right side of the screen. Press Enter to be taken to a "Summer 1986" screen with three movie trailers for you to enjoy: *Aliens, Big Trouble in Little China,* and *The Fly.*

Now go back to the "Special Features" menu and select "DVD Production Credits" at the bottom of the screen. Once inside, click Enter to scroll through the pages of credits, and eventually you'll be treated to eight screen shots from the "Big Trouble in Little China" Commodore 64 computer game. Man, have graphics changed!

Blade II

New Line Cinema ★ **Released** 2002 ★ **Directed by** Guillermo del Toro ★
Starring Wesley Snipes, Kris Kristofferson, Ron Perlman, Leonor Varela,
Norman Reedus, Luke Goss

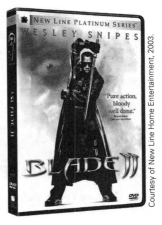

Courtesy of New Line Home Entertainment, 2003.

A new breed of vampire is threatening the world, so Blade (Wesley Snipes) forms an alliance with an elite team of Bloodpack vampires to stop the more ravenous Reapers.

Pop in the second disc and select the first entry, entitled "Production Workshop." Now scroll down and select "Visual Effects." Once inside, highlight the words "Progress Reports" but don't press Enter—instead, tap the Right Arrow on the DVD remote and then the Up Arrow. A red symbol will appear on the right-hand side of the screen. Press Enter to watch a humorous clip with director Guillermo del Toro having some fun....

There's another small egg: Also on the second disc, scroll down to highlight the words "Promotional Material" but don't press Enter just yet. Instead, tap the Left Arrow and a secret gray New Line logo in the corner of the screen will appear. Press Enter to read the six pages of DVD production credits.

The Blair Witch Project

Artisan ★ **Released** 1999 ★ **Directed by** Daniel Myrick, Eduardo Sánchez ★
Starring Heather Donahue, Michael Williams, Joshua Leonard

Courtesy of Artisan Home Entertainment Inc.

You remember the premise behind this mega-successful independent horror film: In October of 1994, three student filmmakers disappeared in the woods near Burkittsville, Maryland, while shooting a documentary... a year later their footage was found.

Pop in the DVD and from the main menu, head to the section "Special Features" (the last option on the screen). Now, instead of selecting from this list, press the Right Arrow on the DVD remote, and a large yellow Blair Witch stick figure will appear in the bottom-right corner of the screen.

Press Enter to watch a trailer for *The Blair Witch Project,* two extra teaser trailers for the film, and a bonus trailer for Stephen King's *The Stand,* a DVD featuring the six-hour made-for-TV movie.

Blair Witch 2: The Book of Shadows

Artisan Entertainment ★ Released 2000 ★ **Directed by** Joe Berlinger ★ **Starring** Kim Director, Jeffrey Donovan, Erica Leerhsen, Tristine Skyler, Stephen Barker Turner

Four young fans of the original Blair Witch movie decide to visit Burkittsville, Maryland, and spend the night in creepy Rustin Parr house. The next day, the college students realize the footage they shot on camera doesn't exactly gel with their memory from the night before.

The DVD is chock-full of hidden features.

Courtesy of Artisan Home Entertainment Inc.

From the main menu, select "Scene Index" and press Enter. Tap the Right Arrow to access the first of many rune symbols peppered throughout this DVD, giving more insight into the Blair Witch mythology. Press Enter to read up on the significance of this rune.

Additional runes can be found by entering the "Chapters 1–4" area of the "Scene Index" section (here, press the Left Arrow on the remote), and another rune is found in the "Audio Features" section by pressing the Right Arrow three times.

More can be found in the "DVD-ROM Materials" section, the "Production Notes" area, and the "Cast & Crew" pages.

There's another egg. Visit the "Audio Features" section, and once inside, highlight the "Priority Records" tab and press Enter to unlock a secret live video featuring the band GodHead.

Lastly, while it's not quite an Easter egg, *Blair Witch 2: The Book of Shadows* is the first disc to deliver a DVD movie on one side and a full music CD on the other side (which can be played in any CD player).

Enjoy!

Blow

New Line Cinema ★ Released 2001 **★ Directed by** Ted Demme **★ Starring**
Johnny Depp, Penélope Cruz

In this true story, George Jung (Johnny Depp) becomes the largest importer of Columbian cocaine to the United States in the '70s and '80s. This film chronicles the rise and fall of his career and examines Jung's relationship with drug lord Pablo Escobar (Cliff Curtis) and his wife, Mirtha (Penélope Cruz).

On this DVD, scroll down to the bottom over the words "Need Help?" but don't press Enter just yet. Instead, press the Right Arrow, and a New Line Cinema Infinifilm logo will appear on the lower-right corner of the screen.

Press Enter for ten pages of DVD credits. Yes, it takes that many people to create a good DVD these days!

Blue Velvet: Special Edition

MGM ★ Released 1986 **★ Directed by** David Lynch **★ Starring** Kyle
MacLachlan, Isabella Rossellini, Dennis Hopper, Laura Dern

Leave it to David Lynch to dig below the surface of a seemingly quiet American town and expose a dark and disturbing underworld.

On this "Special Edition" DVD, some Easter eggs also lie below the surface.

From the main menu, scroll down, and a blue picket fence will appear over a video clip at the bottom of the screen. Press Enter and then all the video clips on the main menu page will change to four new ones. Scroll down once again and a blue bird will appear over the second video clip. Press Enter and it'll turn red just before launching a behind-the-scenes interview on how the filmmakers found the robin for the movie. Interesting tale!

Now, from the main menu, select "Special Features" and use the remote to scroll up once.

The word "Special" in "Special Features" will turn red. Press Enter to hear David Lynch divulge his unhealthy eating habits.

Also from the "Special Features" menu, select the first entry, "Documentary: The Mysteries of Love." Instead of selecting from this list of chapters, press the Up Arrow, and the words "Mysteries of Love" will turn red. Now press Enter to watch an interview clip featuring actress Isabella Rossellini, who talks about the accusations of Lynch being a misogynist.

But wait—there's one more. From the main menu, choose the "Scene Selections" section, and by pressing the Left Arrow or Right Arrow, you'll see a blue ear appear in between sections 3 and 4. Press Enter for additional interview footage, this time with Kyle MacLachlan, who chats about the origins of his silly "Chicken Walk" scene (also shown here).

Boogie Nights: Special Edition

New Line Cinema ★ Released 1997 **★ Directed by** Paul Thomas Anderson ★ **Starring** Mark Wahlberg, Julianne Moore, Burt Reynolds, Don Cheadle, John C. Reilly, William H. Macy, Heather Graham, Nicole Parker, Philip Seymour Hoffman

It's the late 1970s and porn director Jack Horner (Burt Reynolds) discovers an aspiring actor, Eddie Adams (Mark Wahlberg), and transforms him into Dirk Diggler. Thanks to Diggler's "gift" and determination, he becomes a star in the adult-film industry—but of course, fame and fortune have a price, as Adams soon realizes.

Pop in the first disc from this "Special Edition" set, and from the main menu, select the "Setup" screen and then choose "Color Bars." This will take you to those familiar TV color bars to adjust your set, but wait 15 seconds or so, and you'll be treated to an outtake of the adult awards ceremony. Actor Robert Ridgely (who plays "Colonel James" in the movie) apparently ad-libbed much of this hilarious sequence.

After this clip, be forewarned—there's a few minutes of the "Diggler" in the raw with his, er, prosthetic penis. (Note: This is likely not Wahlberg, as the body's face is cut off from view in this extended version of the memorable scene from the movie.)

Now put in the second DVD, scroll over to the small black New Line Cinema logo, and press Enter. This will take you to the DVD credits for this two-disc set.

Bowfinger

Universal Studios ★ Released 1999 ★ **Directed by** Frank Oz ★ **Starring** Steve Martin, Eddie Murphy, Heather Graham

B obby Bowfinger (Steve Martin), a down-and-out movie director, must find a way to get Hollywood's biggest celebrity, Kit Ramsey (Eddie Murphy), to star, against his wishes, in a film. How does he achieve this? With the help of Kit's nerdy look-alike brother, Jiff (Eddie Murphy), and an ambitious wannabe, Daisy (Heather Graham).

©1999 Universal City Studios Inc.

Thankfully, this DVD isn't as low budget as *Cubby Rain*, the film they're making in *Bowfinger*. While not quite an Easter egg, a handful of undocumented trailers to other Universal films appear on this DVD.

From the main menu, select "Bonus Materials," click Enter to access the second page, and scroll down to select "Recommendations."

Over these next two pages, there are trailers to *Liar Liar, The Nutty Professor*, and *EDtv*.

But wait—there's one more.

Go back to the "Recommendations" page, and scroll up to "Universal Showcase" to watch a dramatic movie trailer to *Hurricane* starring Denzel Washington as Rubin "Hurricane" Carter.

Is This a Croc or What?

W hile there was a script written for the film, *The Crocodile Hunter: Collision Course,* (page 38) husband and wife Steve and Terri Irwin ad-libbed much of the entire film—just like in the hit TV show! And, of course, Steve performed all of his own stunts. Would you expect anything less?

Bride of Chucky

Universal Pictures ★ Released 1998 **★ Directed by** Ronny Yu **★ Starring**
Jennifer Tilly, Brad Dourif, Katherine Heigl, Nick Stable, John Ritter

The tortured soul of a serial killer has been trapped inside a doll (which he uses to do his bidding). In this sequel, Chucky's former flame (Jennifer Tilly) rescues the doll pieces from a police compound, resurrects him, and eventually joins him as a fellow pint-sized killer.

From the main menu, scroll down and select "Bonus Materials" and then choose "Cast & Filmmakers." Now choose "Brad Dourif" (the voice of Chucky) and press the Right Arrow to peruse his bio and filmography. On the second-to-last page, you'll notice a film reel by *Child's Play 2* (1990). Use the DVD remote to navigate over to it, and press Enter to watch an undocumented trailer for the film.

The Bride of Frankenstein

Universal Studios ★ Released 1935 **★ Directed by** James Whale **★ Starring**
Boris Karloff, Colin Clive, Ernest Thesiger

She's alive!

One of the most acclaimed horror classics in movie-making history (and a sequel to *Frankenstein*, released four years earlier), this bizarre tale returns Dr. Frankenstein (Colin Clive) as the scientist who must create a mate for everyone's favorite square-headed monster, Frankenstein (Boris Karloff).

Their courtship doesn't go quite as planned.

On the DVD, select "Bonus Materials" from the main menu, and then scroll down to select "Cast & Filmmakers" (second choice from the bottom).

Select the first entry—"Boris Karloff as The Monster"—and scroll to the seventh page using the Right Arrow on the remote. You'll notice there's a small word "Preview" beside "Frankenstein." Press the Up Arrow on the remote until the word turns green, and then press Enter to watch a special treat—the original 1931 trailer to the film *Frankenstein*.

The same exciting trailer can be seen on the fourth page under director James Whale's biography/filmography, also in the "Cast & Filmmakers" section.

Bring It On

Universal Pictures ★ Released 2000 ★ **Directed by** Peyton Reed ★ **Starring** Kirsten Dunst, Eliza Dushku, Jesse Bradford, Gabrielle Union

The Rancho Carne High School cheerleading team thought they'd snag the national championships once again—that is, until newly elected team captain Torrance Shipman (Kirsten Dunst) discovers their routine was lifted from a hot hip-hop squad across town. With little time to spare, the cheerleaders need to come up with some new moves for the competition.

From the disc's main menu, scroll over to "Languages" and press Enter. On this new screen, continuously press the Right Arrow on the remote until the yellow cheerleading cone in the lower-right corner of the screen turns red.

Now press Enter and the film's director, Peyton Reed, will appear with this humorous message: "Hey! You found it! The Easter egg! You probably were expecting a really beautiful cheerleader but instead you got me—a skinny, pathetic director. Nice job!"

The 'Burbs

Universal Studios ★ Released 1989 ★ **Directed by** Joe Dante ★ **Starring** Tom Hanks, Bruce Dern, Carrie Fisher

Tom Hanks portrays suburbanite Ray Peterson, whose vacation-at-home goes awry when he and his wacky neighbors—a paranoid ex-soldier, a hefty busybody, and a spaced-out teenager—begin to investigate the strange happenings next door at Dr. Klopek's residence. Needless to say, Peterson's vacation proves to be anything but relaxing.

Here's a bit o' trivia: in the Klopek's house, the sled is named "Rosebud," an obvious nod to *Citizen Kane,* and their dog is named "Landru," a likely reference to Henri "Bluebeard" Landru, the infamous French serial killer.

The DVD for this suspenseful comedy has an undocumented alternate ending— from the main menu, select "Bonus Materials" and then select the "Alternate Ending" option at the top of the screen.

Enjoy this never-before-released ten-minute clip as Peterson is saved from Dr. Werner Klopek (Henry Gibson) before the ambulance takes off.

Carrie

MGM ★ Released 1976 ★ **Directed by** Brian De Palma ★ **Starring** Sissy Spacek, John Travolta, Piper Laurie

"If *The Exorcist* made you shudder, *Carrie* will make you scream" was one of the taglines for this chilling horror flick about a teenage outcast with special powers. She gets pushed too far on prom night, and as you can imagine, the evening turns into a, er, bloody mess.

Carrie was Stephen King's first novel-turned-film in 1976, followed by *Salem's Lot* in 1979 (a made-for-TV movie) and *The Shining* in 1980.

If you have the guts to watch this nail-biting thriller all the way through, perhaps you'll also have the stomach for a little-known image at the very end?

Let the credits roll (or fast forward through them), and after the screen goes black, you'll be treated to a still shot of a bloody Carrie with her mom peeking behind the door....

Did You Know?

The "blood" that was dumped on Carrie White (Sissy Spacek) in the climactic prom scene was actually gallons of corn syrup and food coloring.

Casablanca

Warner Bros. ★ **Released** 1942 ★ **Directed by** Michael Curtiz ★ **Starring** Humphrey Bogart, Ingrid Bergman, Paul Henreid

This film tells the tale of an exiled American, Rick Blaine (Humphrey Bogart), who runs the hottest nightclub in Casablanca during World War II. Ingrid Bergman stars as Ilsa Lund, Blaine's ex-lover who deserted him in Paris. She comes to the nightclub as the companion of an underground leader, Victor Laszlo (Paul Henreid)—with Germans on their tail.

Since its original theatrical release in 1942, the film spawned countless lousy Bogart impressions for generations to come. Here's looking at you, kid.

Although the Easter eggs in this classic film aren't too hard to find, they are indeed undocumented extras, and a special treat, too.

From the main menu of the movie, select the "Special Features" page. You'll find eight movie trailers: *The Petrified Forest, High Sierra, The Maltese Falcon, Passage to Marseille, To Have and Have Not, The Big Sleep, Treasure of the Sierra Madre,* and *Key Largo.*

Sit back and enjoy.

Cast Away

20th Century Fox ★ **Released** 2000 ★ **Directed by** Robert Zemeckis ★ **Starring** Tom Hanks

FedEx systems engineer Chuck Noland (Tom Hanks) washes up on a deserted island after a harrowing plane crash. With hope, determination, and an instinct for survival, Noland overcomes physical and emotional adversities and plans his escape off the island.

Insert the second (that is, "Supplemental") disc, and then select "Video and Stills Galleries" from the main menu. Use the remote to scroll down to the words "Raft Escape"—but instead of pressing Enter, tap the Left Arrow on the remote, and a set of yellow and blue wings will appear toward the left of the screen. Now press Enter.

As the text explains on this page, on March 13, 2001, director Robert Zemeckis participated in a Q&A at the USC School of Cinema and Television. One student asked the director what was in the unopened FedEx package Noland carried around with him throughout the movie. If you press "Play," you'll hear his response, followed by laughter and applause.

Cats & Dogs

Warner Bros. ★ **Released** 2001 ★ **Directed by** Lawrence Guterman ★ **Starring** Jeff Goldblum, Elizabeth Perkins, Alexander Pollock

In this unlikely "tail," a young beagle named Lou is out to stop a cunning cat from enslaving all of humanity.

If you get your paws on this DVD, select the word "Cats" from the main menu, and then scroll down four times until a red block at the bottom of the screen turns white. Press Enter to play a hidden trivia game. You're asked three questions (and the correct answer for each is "Cats"), prompting a cute graphic that says "Congratulations: Proceed to Cat Headquarters."

Here's another egg: While still in the "Cats" portion of the DVD, select "Special Features" and then press the Down Arrow on the remote until the cat's prickly toy is highlighted on the left of the screen. Press Enter to watch Mr. Tinkles' screen tests for other (fake) films including parodies of *Apocalypse Now, The Terminator, The Sixth Sense,* and *Forrest Gump.* Wait to the very end for a cute surprise!

On the second page of "Special Features," scroll down three times until the image of the cat turns red. Press Enter to watch some "frisky" clips from *Cats & Dogs.*

Now eject the DVD and start it again, this time choosing "Dogs" from the main menu. Press the Down Arrow four times, and a white block at the bottom of the screen will turn blue. Press Enter and play this trivia game, with all the answers being "Dog," prompting another "Congratulations!" screen with a graphic.

Now select "Special Features" and scroll down three times until the tube in the middle of the screen turns pale blue. Press Enter to enjoy some concept sketches for the film.

Lastly, go to the second "Special Features" page, and scroll down three times until the emblem turns another color. Now press Enter to watch some "doggone" clips from the film.

Top Films as Chosen by You

According to voters at the Internet Movie Database (www.imdb .com), one of the most popular destinations on the Internet for movie lovers, the top 20 movies of all time are as follows:

1. The Godfather
2. The Shawshank Redemption
3. The Godfather: Part II
4. The Lord of the Rings: The Fellowship of the Ring
5. Schindler's List
6. Casablanca
7. Citizen Kane
8. Shichinin no samurai
9. Star Wars
10. Dr. Strangelove or: How I Learned to Stop Worrying and Love the Bomb
11. One Flew over the Cuckoo's Nest
12. The Lord of the Rings: The Two Towers,
13. Memento
14. Rear Window
15. Star Wars: Episode V—The Empire Strikes Back
16. Raiders of the Lost Ark
17. The Usual Suspects
18. Pulp Fiction
19. Le Fabuleux destin d'Amélie Poulain
20. North by Northwest

Charlie's Angels

Columbia Pictures ★ Released 2000 ★ **Directed** by McG (a.k.a. Joseph McGinty Nichol) ★ **Starring** Cameron Diaz, Drew Barrymore, Lucy Liu, Bill Murray, Tim Curry, John Forsythe, Crispin Glover

Based on the over-the-top 70s TV action series of the same name, *Charlie's Angels* stars three sexy detectives who work for a mysterious boss, Charlie.

The trio must use their brains, looks, driving skills, and martial arts abilities to stop a pair of evil computer hackers. Fun fluff indeed.

There are three Easter eggs hidden on this DVD. From the main menu go to the "Special Features" section and highlight "Getting G'd Up." Don't press Enter— instead, tap the Right Arrow on the remote and Diaz' midsection will be highlighted. Now press Enter for a sexy montage of all three Angels.

Next, go to the second page of "Special Features" and select "Wired Angels." Press the Left Arrow and then Enter to watch as Barrymore undergoes painstaking plaster masking.

Lastly, on the third "Special Features" page, highlight the little arrow at the bottom of the screen and instead of pressing Enter, tap the Right Arrow on the remote to bring up an extensive video of outtakes and rehearsals (and an impressive Christopher Walken impression by Sam Rockwell!).

Charlotte's Web

Paramount Pictures ★ Released 1973 ★ **Directed by** Charles A. Nichols, Iwao Takamoto ★ **Starring** Debbie Reynolds, Paul Lynde, Henry Gibson, Agnes Moorehead

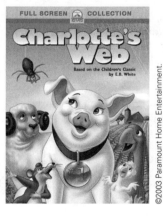

In this classic children's tale from E.B. White, Charlotte the spider (Debbie Reynolds) teaches Wilbur the pig (Henry Gibson), Templeton the rat (Paul Lynde), and other animals the meaning of friendship and love.

Want to know how to unlock the secret Easter egg? From the main menu, select the "Special Features" submenu and press Enter to go inside. Once there, choose the "Meet the Animals Game" option. After the narration, the game will start. Select any of the animals, such as the rat, horse, pig, or owl (it doesn't matter which one) and press the Up Arrow to highlight the tiny Charlotte in the corner of the screen. Press Enter to read random facts about spiders. Did you know that spiders are not insects? They are arachnids. They have eight legs, four to eight eyes, and a pair of spinnerets to make their webs! Try this Easter egg with all of the animals!

Chasing Amy: The Criterion Collection

Miramax/Buena Vista Home Entertainment ★ **Released** 1997 ★ **Directed by** Kevin Smith ★ **Starring** Ben Affleck, Joey Lauren Adams, Jason Lee, Dwight Ewell, Jason Mewes, Kevin Smith

Comic-book artist Holden McNeil (Ben Affleck) falls in love with fellow artist (and lesbian) Alyssa Jones (Joey Lauren Adams), threatening their friendship and his work relationship with his business partner, Banky Edwards (Jason Lee).

This special edition "Criterion Collection" DVD houses a number of extras designed for fans of Kevin Smith's film.

From the disc's main menu, the last option on this screen is "Color Bars"—you know, the color-bar test pattern as seen on TV. Before the color bars start, listen as Smith, Affleck, Scott Mosier, and Jason Mewes joke around, and then again during the color bars, and again at the end of them.

Typical silliness from Kevin Smith and company!

Chicken Run

DreamWorks Pictures ★ **Released** 2000 ★ **Directed by** Peter Lord, Nick Park ★ **Starring** Mel Gibson, Julia Sawalha, Lynn Ferguson, Jane Horrocks, Phil Daniels, Timothy Spall, Tony Haygarth, Miranda Richardson, Imelda Staunton, Benjamin Whitrow

This hilarious animated film chronicles the lives of confined chickens who decide to fly the coop with the help of a smooth-talking American rooster, Rocky Rhodes (Mel Gibson).

You'll find a dozen eggs in *Chicken Run* (fitting, huh?).

These cracked-egg images—when found and accessed on this DVD— reveal some neat facts about the feature film.

For example, from the main menu, select the "Audio" option, scroll down to the words "2.0 Digital Surround," but don't press Enter. Instead, press the Down

Arrow again, and an orange cracked egg will appear in the middle of the screen. Press Enter to read a random fun fact.

One of the factoids says: "There are 100 stages in the process of making an average chicken. Each stage is divided into the following processes: body, armature, fluffles (feathers), legs, head, beak, comb, cowl, wings, tail, necklace, color and eyes."

There are 11 other orange and green eggs hidden elsewhere on these DVD menus—see how many you can find. You can find them here:

- Audio menu—below "2.0 Dolby Digital"
- Subtitles menu—above "Main Menu"
- Special Features menu—above "Main Menu"
- Trailers and TV Spots menu—to the right of "TV Spot"
- Production Notes menu—on page 5 beside the Back icon
- Mel Gibson menu in the "Cast" section—above the word "Bios"
- Tony Haygarth menu in the "Cast" section—page 2, above "Bios"
- Jane Horrocks menu in the "Cast" section—page 2, by the Back icon
- Imelda Staunton menu in the "Cast" section—above "Bios"
- Loyd Price menu in the "Crew" section—page 2, by the Back icon
- Dave Alex Riddett in the "Crew" section—above "Bios"
- Scene Index—between Scenes 17 and 18

If you want to read all 12 factoids without trying to find all the eggs, simply reenter eggs you've found (in the Audio submenu, for example), and each factoid should be randomly generated, thus different. Eventually, you'll read all of them.

Another fun thing to do on this DVD: Click the "Panic Button" icon from the main menu and "Special Features" menu to watch several different clips of the hens screaming!

Lastly, the "Sneak Preview" inside the Trailer and TV Spots menu is of DreamWorks' blockbuster *Shrek*.

Citizen Kane

Warner Bros. ★ **Released** 1941 ★ **Directed by** Orson Welles ★ **Starring** Orson Welles, Joseph Cotten, Dorothy Comingore, Agnes Moorehead, George Coulouris, Ruth Warrick, Ray Collins

In Orson Welles' masterpiece, which was nominated for a Best Picture award in 1942 (but lost out to *How Green Was My Valley*), multimillionaire newspaper tycoon Charles Foster Kane dies alone, uttering a single word, "Rosebud." This film chronicles the sensational life of Kane, examines his personal and professional affairs, and sheds light on the meaning of his dying word.

On the DVD, visit the "Special Features" page from the main menu, and then tap the Right Arrow on your DVD remote. A "Rosebud" sled will appear—press Enter to be treated to a five-minute interview with actress Ruth Warrick (who plays Emily Kane in the film).

The second egg can be found in the "Production Notes" area. From here, visit the "In the Beginning" section and then choose "Still Galleries." By selecting the sleds, you will unlock hidden interviews with editor Robert Wise and film critic Roger Ebert.

The Crocodile Hunter: Collision Course

MGM ★ **Released** 2002 ★ **Directed by** John Stainton ★ **Starring** Steve Irwin, Terri Irwin, Magda Szubanski, David Wenham

Crikey! This TV-turned-movie franchise follows Steve Irwin (as himself) on a mission to save a crocodile from poachers—little does he know the reptile has swallowed something valuable to the U.S. government! Don't try these death-defying stunts at home!

There are three Easter eggs to be found on this DVD. From the main menu, simply press the Left Arrow and the left video section at the bottom of the screen will become illuminated. Press Enter to view a four-minute interview clip with camera operator Tony Politis about what it's like to convert a popular TV franchise into a motion picture.

Next, go back to the main menu and select the "Special Features" section. Once inside, press the Up Arrow on the DVD remote and the word "Features" at the top of the screen will now be underlined. Press Enter to watch another hidden interview clip—this time with Jean Turnbull, the film's costume designer, about the biggest challenge in working on this kind of film.

Last, from the main menu, select "Scene Selections." Now navigate over to the "Scenes 9-12" section, and then highlight scene number 9, "Nurturers." Don't press Enter—instead, press the Up Arrow on the DVD remote and the word "Scene" at the top of the page will become illuminated. Now press Enter to watch yet another secret video clip. This time it's about the movie's stunt work on water. Speaking on camera about halfway through the clip is Chris Anderson, the film's stunt coordinator.

Dances with Wolves: Special Edition

MGM ★ Released 1990 ★ **Directed by** Kevin Costner ★ **Starring** Kevin Costner, Mary McDonnell, Graham Greene, Rodney A. Grant

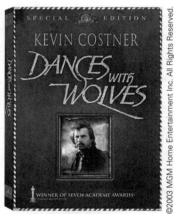

In this Oscar-winning post-Civil War drama, a lone Union Army soldier (Kevin Costner) befriends a Native American tribe at the risk of becoming an enemy of the white man.

There's a hidden Easter egg planted on this disc—if you know how to find it. Pop in the second DVD ("Special Features") and, from the main menu, press the Up Arrow on the DVD remote. The shadow of a wolf will appear under the words "Dances with Wolves." Press Enter to see some behind-the-scenes footage via a presentation reel from editor Neil Travis. A rare, five-minute treat!

Dante's Peak: Collector's Edition

Universal Pictures ★ Released 1997 **★ Directed by** Roger Donaldson ★
Starring Pierce Brosnan, Linda Hamilton

Dr. Harry Dalton (Pierce Brosnan) and Dante's Peak mayor Rachel Wando (Linda Hamilton) believe a dormant volcano is about to erupt, threatening the lives and homes of this peaceful town.

This "Collector's Edition" DVD features production design sketches, a look into the special effects of the film, trailers and posters, the shooting script, and of course, an Easter egg.

From the main menu, select "Bonus Materials" and then choose "Getting Close to the Show: The Making of Dante's Peak."

Once inside, select "Language Selection" and then "Spoken Language." Scroll down and press Enter over the words "Musical Score" and then over "Return to Movie" to watch this hour-long documentary with just the score.

Dark City

New Line Cinema ★ Released 1998 **★ Directed by** Alex Proyas **★ Starring** Rufus Sewell, Kiefer Sutherland, Jennifer Connelly, Richard O'Brien, Ian Richardson, William Hurt

From the director of *The Crow* comes this twisted tale starring Rufus Sewell as John Murdoch, who awakens in a hotel room to find himself wanted for a series of brutal murders.

Along with the widescreen and full screen versions of the film, a hidden game is also on the *Dark City* DVD.

From the main menu, select "Special Features" and then scroll down to the last entry, "To Shell Beach…" Once inside, read the rules for the game.

Need a spoiler? OK, here's how to solve it if you're stuck:

To find the bloody knife, go back to the "Special Features" menu, and select the first entry, "Cast & Crew." Now go to the "Kiefer Sutherland" biography, and once inside, press the Right Arrow two times; when a gray knife appears at the bottom of the screen, press Enter.

Now go back to the "Special Features" menu, and select "Neil Gaiman on Dark City." Once inside, press the Up Arrow and a blue business card will appear. Press Enter and the card will turn orange, leading you to more info.

Go back to the "Special Features" menu, and select the option "The Metropolis Comparison." Scroll down and choose "Original Weekly Variety Review," and scroll to the last page. When there, press the Up Arrow to highlight the postcard from Shell Beach and then press Enter.

Now go back to the "Cast & Crew" screen, and enter the biography of Trevor Jones on the second page. Now click "More" until you land on the tenth and final page of this biography, and press the Up Arrow to highlight the Shell Beach souvenir. Press Enter.

Go back to the "Cast & Crew" section and choose "William Hurt." Click "More" during his bio until the eighth and final page. Press the Up Arrow to highlight the clock and press Enter.

Finally, go back to the "Special Features" menu and choose "Set Designs" (second from the top). Once inside, click the word "More" until you land on the picture of the syringe. Press the Up Arrow and press Enter.

If you complete this Easter egg hunt in the correct sequence, you'll be treated to a very strange and psychedelic animated sequence.

The disc also contains two hidden video clips:

From the main menu, scroll down and choose "Special Features," and then press Enter to choose the first entry, "Cast & Crew." Now select "Kiefer Sutherland" and select the word "More" three times. An undocumented video clip from *Twin Peaks: Fire Walk with Me,* also starring Sutherland, will appear.

Now visit the William Hurt biography, and do the same thing—press "More" five times until you see a clickable *Lost in Space* clip featuring Hurt.

Death to Smoochy

Warner Bros. ★ **Released** 2002 ★ **Directed by** Danny DeVito ★ **Starring** Robin Williams, Ed Norton, Danny DeVito

In this underrated comedy, a washed-up children's TV star (Robin Williams) plots his vengeful return when the network chooses a clean-as-a-whistle replacement (Ed Norton) to take over the TV show. Very funny flick indeed!

And of course, there's a funny Easter egg to find, too. From the main menu, select "Special Features" (second from the bottom) and then choose "Continue" to enter the submenu. Once inside, navigate to the bottom of the screen and highlight the words "Main Menu" but don't press Enter. Instead, press the Up Arrow on the DVD remote and the chalk outline on the ground will become illuminated. Now press Enter to watch a very humorous outtake with Robin Williams and Ed Norton cracking up during a car scene. It's hilarious to see two professionals who can't stop laughing….

Detroit Rock City

New Line Entertainment ★ **Released** 1999 ★ **Directed by** Adam Rifkin ★ **Starring** Edward Furlong, Giuseppe Andrews, James DeBello, Sam Huntington

Part road-trip flick, part coming of age story, this film takes place in 1978, when a high school rock band from Cleveland decides to travel to Detroit to pay homage to the greatest rock and roll band alive, KISS.

From the main menu of this DVD, scroll up until the small New Line logo is highlighted with the green stripe. Press Enter to go to an interactive credits screen. Press Enter over the first entry for "Angry Monkey," the folks responsible for the menu design on the DVD.

Select "More" to go to the second page. Now press Enter over the word "Facts" in the bottom-right corner of the screen. This will launch the silly yet entertaining video clip entitled "Facts," an Angry Monkey tale. Press Enter to go from one screen to the next.

Now head back to the credits section, and select "Three Legged Cat Productions," the team responsible for the commentaries and featurettes. Click "More" four times until the last page of "Special Thanks." Press Enter over the word "The Devil Roosevelt" for the picture of the band.

Lastly, go back and select "Tim Sullivan" at the bottom of the screen for a picture of him with the four KISS members in makeup.

Devil's Advocate

Warner Bros. ★ **Released** 1997 ★ **Directed by** Taylor Hackford ★ **Starring** Keanu Reeves, Al Pacino, Charlize Theron, Jeffrey Jones, Judith Ivey, Craig T. Nelson

Kevin Lomax (Keanu Reeves) is a hotshot lawyer who has never lost a case— but he's about to lose his soul if the Devil himself (Al Pacino) has his way. In fact, ol' Satan has a lot more in store for Lomax, whether he's ready for it or not.

Movie fans will get a kick out of the five hidden Warner Brothers theatrical trailers on this disc. Here's how to find them: Pop in the DVD and then select "Recommendations" near the bottom of the screen. Once inside, select the entry entitled "Genre." Enjoy trailers to these supernatural thrillers: *The Exorcist* (1973), *Interview with a Vampire* (1994), *Lady Hawke* (1985), and *The Witches of Eastwick* (1987).

Die Hard: Five Star Collection

20th Century Fox ★ **Released** 1988 ★
Directed by John McTiernan ★
Starring Bruce Willis

Gutsy NYPD cop John McClane (Bruce Willis) flies to L.A. to spend Christmas with his estranged wife, but her holiday office party comes to an abrupt end when bond-stealing European terrorists lock down the high-rise building and take hostages as collateral.

Insert the second disc from this popular action flick, and instead of choosing from any of these bonus features, press the Up Arrow

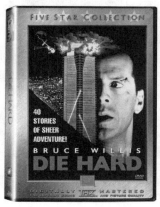

on the remote twice, and a red light will illuminate at the top middle of the helicopter landing pad.

Press Enter and before you know it, the high-rise building will blow up, followed by the words, "There Goes Fox Home Entertainment!"

On the same disc, select "From The Vault" from the main menu and then choose "Outtakes." Now select "The Vault." Once inside, press the Right Arrow twice, and a small white gun will appear on the screen. Press Enter and the gun will turn yellow before launching some outtakes from the film. (Note: There is music, but no dialogue.)

A less exciting egg is on the first disc. From the main menu, go to the "Language Selection" screen. Scroll down over the word "English" (under "Subtitles"), but do not press Enter just yet. Instead, press the Right Arrow, and a light will shine off the left side of Bruce Willis' face. Now press Enter to access a hidden DVD credits screen.

Die Hard 2: Die Harder

20th Century Fox ★ Released 1990 ★ **Directed by** Renny Harlin ★ **Starring** Bruce Willis

Renegade terrorists seize a major international airport on Christmas Eve, holding thousands of holiday travelers hostage. Off-duty cop John McClane (Bruce Willis), who is experiencing somewhat of a déjà vu for this time of year, is determined to save the day (once again!).

This "Special Edition" double DVD (also found in the *Die Hard* Trilogy Box Set) features a number of making-of documentaries, featurettes, deleted scenes, storyboards, interviews, trailers, and TV spots.

There's a small egg, too.

Insert the second DVD ("Special Features"). From the main menu, scroll all the way to the bottom, and highlight the words "Visual Effects," but without pressing Enter just yet. Instead, tap the Right Arrow on the DVD remote, and the railing will turn white. Press Enter to read four full pages of DVD credits for the making of this collector's edition DVD set.

Die Hard with a Vengeance

20th Century Fox ★ Released 1995 **★ Directed by** John McTiernan **★ Starring**
Bruce Willis, Jeremy Irons, Samuel L. Jackson

Bruce Willis reprises his role as tough cop John McClane, who is now the target of the mysterious Simon (Jeremy Irons), a deadly terrorist hell-bent on blowing up the city of New York if he doesn't get what he wants. McClane is joined by an unwilling civilian, Zeus Carver (Samuel L. Jackson).

On the second DVD, select "Interview and Profile" from the main menu. Once inside, press the Left Arrow on the DVD remote, and the "Exit" sign in the subway will illuminate in white. Press Enter for an enjoyable collage of outtakes from the film.

"I'll get this right," smirks Willis, embarrassed, in one scene. In another, Jackson laughs and swears when Willis fouls up another line.

Now head back to the main menu, and highlight the words "Trailers and TV Spots," but do not press Enter. Instead, press the Right Arrow, and the subway post on the right side of the screen will glow white. Press Enter to read the credits for the DVD.

Dinosaur

Walt Disney Pictures ★ Released 2000 **★ Directed by** Eric Leighton, Ralph Zondag **★ Starring** D.B. Sweeney, Alfre Woodard, Ossie Davis, Max Casella, Hayden Panettiere, Samuel E. Wright, Julianna Margulies, Peter Siragusa, Joan Plowright, Della Reese

Step back in time to an age where dinosaurs ruled the Earth. After a meteorite shower destroys his home, an orphaned dinosaur, Aladar, goes on an epic, eye-opening journey.

Disney's *Dinosaur* is a technical marvel that's perfect for kids and adults alike.

Along with the many features on this two-disc DVD set is a handful of eggs.

Pop in the second disc and press the Left Arrow. The small sticky-note in the bottom-left corner of the screen will change to "DVD Credits." Press Enter to read four pages of who's responsible for this remarkable double-disc set.

Go back to the main menu, and select the first entry, "Development." Once inside, press the Right Arrow and the dinosaur's skull will illuminate in red. Press Enter to watch a lengthy black-and-white video showing Walt Disney chatting about the history of animating dinosaurs, highlighting the work of Windsor McCay, the famous newspaper cartoonist and his classic animation, "Gertie the Dinosaur."

Go back to the main menu, and select the second section, "Creating the Characters." Once again, tap the Right Arrow, and the dinosaur skull will turn red. Press Enter to watch a minute-and-a-half featurette of digital *Dinosaur* outtakes.

Now head back to the main menu, and scroll down to the third section, "The Production Process." Once inside, press the Right Arrow, and the dinosaur's skull will turn red. Press Enter to view a five-minute video featuring Walt Disney and three dinosaurs. This clip originally aired in 1964 to promote the New York World's Fair.

Lastly, return to the main menu, and choose the last section, "Publicity." Once inside, press the Right Arrow again; then press Enter and the dino skull will turn red. This will launch a 12-minute educational cartoon, "Recycle Rex," starring an environmentally friendly dinosaur!

Dirty Dancing: Collector's Edition

Artisan ★ Released 1987 ★ **Directed by** Emile Ardolino ★ **Starring** Jennifer Grey, Patrick Swayze, Jerry Orbach, Cynthia Rhodes

Courtesy of Artisan Home Entertainment Inc.

"Have the time of your life" with Frances "Baby" Houseman (Jennifer Grey), who, during a summer camp getaway with her family, falls in love with Johnny Castle (Patrick Swayze), the camp's dance teacher. At night, Castle, Houseman, and other dancers practice "Dirty Dancing."

From the main menu of this "Collector's Edition" DVD, select "Cast & Crew" and then choose the filmography/biography of Patrick Swayze, Jennifer Grey, and *Dirty*

Dancing's director, Emile Ardolino. (Note: Ardolino's bio is on the second page of this section.)

Use the Right Arrow to scroll through the pages of each bio (press Enter over the silhouette to advance to the next screen), and on the last page, the term "Q&A" will appear. Press the Right Arrow so that the "Q&A" turns blue. Now press Enter to read questions directed to that person.

What's hidden is that you can access video clips with their answers by pressing the Up Arrow and pressing Enter when the red ball appears.

Top 20 Worst Movies of All Time?

According to web surfers who voted at the popular Internet Movie Database (www.imdb.com), the following are the top 20 worst movies of all time. Hey, where's *Howard the Duck?*

1. Manos, the Hands of Fate
2. Troll 2
3. Space Mutiny
4. Future War
5. Eegah
6. Hobgoblins
7. Backyard Dogs
8. Santa with Muscles
9. Police Academy: Mission to Moscow
10. Werewolf
11. Glitter
12. Santa Claus Conquers the Martians
13. Leonard Part 6
14. Turbo: A Power Rangers Movie
15. Kazaam
16. Battlefield Earth: A Saga of the Year 3000
17. Lawnmower Man 2: Beyond Cyberspace
18. Hercules in New York
19. Baby Geniuses
20. It's Pat

Donnie Darko

20th Century Fox ★ Released 2001 **★ Directed by** Richard Kelly **★ Starring**
Jake Gyllenhaal, Jena Malone, Drew Barrymore, Mary McDonnell, Katharine Ross,
Patrick Swayze, Noah Wyle

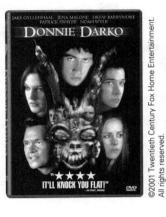

In this underrated psychological thriller, Donnie Darko (Jake Gyllenhaal) is a troubled teen with strange delusions of the past, present, and future. A demonic, man-sized rabbit brings these disturbing, apocalyptic visions to Darko, and he must act on them despite the consequences.

From the main menu of this DVD, scroll to the right using the remote, and enter the "Special Features" submenu. Once inside, select the last entry on this page, "The Philosophy of Time Travel." Now click the Right Arrow to scroll through this book until you reach "Appendix A" (with the picture of the human body on it). Press the Up Arrow once, and a white circle will appear on the man's chest. Now press Enter to watch a deleted scene at a PTA meeting between characters Kitty Farmer (played by Beth Grant) and Karen Pomeroy (Drew Barrymore).

On the second "Appendix" screen—with the image of a man's skeleton facing toward the right—again press the Up Arrow, and the white arrow will turn black. Press Enter to watch the original theatrical trailer to the film.

There's one more egg on this DVD:

Go back out to the "Special Features" menu, and select the option "Cunning Visions." Once inside, scroll down four times until the words "Special Features" are highlighted. Press the Right Arrow and the small rectangular image will now have a white border. Press Enter to view 17 pages of a special web site gallery.

Did You Know?

Actress Jennifer Grey was 27 years old when *Dirty Dancing* (page 46) was filmed, yet her character "Baby" Houseman was supposed to be many years younger.

Lead actor Patrick Swayze sang the hit song from this movie, "She's Like the Wind."

EDtv

Universal Pictures ★ Released 1999 ★ Directed by Ron Howard ★ Starring Matthew McConaughey, Jenna Elfman, Woody Harrelson, Elizabeth Hurley

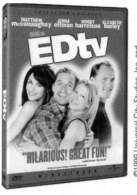

Ed Pekurny (Matthew McConaughey) is a regular guy who becomes the star of a hit reality TV show. His private life becomes a public soap opera spectacle as Ed falls in love with his brother's girlfriend (Jenna Elfman).

From the main menu, scroll up twice and select "Bonus Materials." Then click on the white arrow on the bottom of the screen to enter this section's second page.

Now select "Universal Showcase" to find undocumented trailers to other Universal Studios films including *Bowfinger* and *Mystery Men*.

There are two more trailers on this disc.

On the second page of "Bonus Materials," select "Cast and Filmmakers" and scroll to the second page to select director Ron Howard. On the fourth page of his bio, you'll find a trailer for *Apollo 13*.

Lastly, there's a theatrical trailer for *EDtv* on the second page of "Bonus Materials."

Edward Scissorhands

20th Century Fox ★ Released 1990 ★ Directed by Tim Burton ★ Starring Johnny Depp, Winona Ryder, Dianne Wiest, Anthony Michael Hall, Kathy Baker, Vincent Price, Alan Arkin

Edward (Johnny Depp) lives as a recluse in a castle as an "unfinished invention" and has a peculiar handicap (or gift?): sharp shears for hands. But one sunny day, a kind Avon lady takes him home to live with her suburban family. Tim Burton's *Edward Scissorhands* is a deliciously stylistic "fish-out-of-water" tale that looks and sounds great on DVD.

Here's how to access the Easter egg: From the main menu, go to the "Extra Features" section

and scroll down the list of six options but don't select any of them. Press the Down Arrow one more time and a pair of scissors will appear at the bottom of the screen. Now press Enter and they'll turn yellow before launching into a "special thanks" screen acknowledging folks such as Tim Burton, composer Danny Elfman, and others.

Eight Legged Freaks

Warner Bros. ★ **Released** 2002 ★ **Directed by** Ellory Elkayem ★ **Starring** David Arquette, Kari Wuhrer, Scott Terra, Doug E. Doug, Scarlett Johansson

The only thing worse than a gang of poisonous spiders is when they've mutated into giant eight-legged freaks. That's the premise behind this silly horror/comedy hybrid starring David Arquette and Kari Wuhrer.

This widescreen flick—which pays homage to B-movies from the 1950s—features a handful of DVD extras including an alternate ending, commentary by David Arquette and director/co-writer Ellory Elkayem, theatrical trailers, deleted scenes, and spider trivia.

As a special treat, the DVD also contains Elkayem 's original short film that inspired the movie, dubbed *Larger Than Life*. And of course, the disc also houses an Easter egg. From the main menu select any of the sections (such as "Scenes!" or "Languages!"). Once inside, press the Up Arrow when you see a spider crawling along the screen. When a spider has a target on it, press Enter to read about that particular arachnid. There are five in all. Can you find all the creepy crawlers?

The Evil Dead:
Book of the Dead Edition

Anchor Bay Entertainment ★ **Released** 1982 ★ **Directed by** Sam Raimi ★ **Starring** Bruce Campbell, Ellen Sandweiss, Hal Delrich, Betsy Baker, Sarah York

This must-see classic horror film that launched Bruce "Ash" Campbell as the preeminent cult movie hero tells the tale of five teens who accidentally raise the dead while spending the night in a remote cabin. Don't you hate when that happens?

And as if this cool-looking DVD—with the soft rubber case to resemble the actual "Book of the Dead" from the film—weren't enough to satiate fans, you can also uncover two hidden Easter eggs.

Select "Extras" from the main menu, and instead of picking from this list of options (which includes "Poster and Still Gallery" and "Commentaries"), tap the Left Arrow, and the transparent fish will illuminate on the right side of the screen. Now press Enter to watch a rare, minute-long "Special Make-Up Effects Test" video clip of a zombie's face decaying and bleeding. Lovely!

The second egg can be found once again on the "Extras" page. Choose "More" to be taken to the second batch of options. You may notice two transparent skulls on the screen. Press the Left Arrow, and the left skull will turn blood red. Press Enter to watch a special behind-the-scenes video shot on Halloween 2001 when Anchor Bay Entertainment screened a new print of *The Evil Dead* to a capacity crowd at the American Cinematheque, Hollywood.

The Fast and the Furious

Universal Studios ★ Released 2001 ★ **Directed by** Rob Cohen ★ **Starring** Paul Walker, Vin Diesel

©2001 Universal City Studios, Inc.

Officer Brian O'Conner (Paul Walker) is an undercover cop who infiltrates a gang of L.A. street racers—posing as one of their own daredevil drivers—in order to solve a crime. But O'Connor falls in love with the sister of the ex-con gang leader, Domenic Toretto (Vin Diesel).

Like stunts? Then you'll definitely "flip" over the Easter eggs in this film.

From the main menu, select "Bonus Materials" and then scroll down to "Multiple Camera Angle Stunt Sequence" (second from the bottom). Press the Right Arrow, and a yellow steering wheel will appear on the right side of the screen. Press Enter to watch one of the last car stunts from the film—but from multiple angles. Great stuff.

Back in the "Bonus Materials" screen, select "Racer X: The Article That Inspired The Movie." When this article by Kenneth Li appears on the screen, press the Up Arrow and another yellow steering wheel will appear near the top. Press Enter to watch interviews with cast and crew members, interspersed with video footage from the film.

Also, let the credits roll at the end of the movie to be treated to a scene with Toretto (Diesel) cruising through Baja, Mexico.

Lastly, the DVD has a little-known demo of Activision's "Supercar Street Challenge" computer game embedded on the disc. It offers players two cars and two tracks to race on. It's a fun, arcade-like racing game, and a fitting addition to the fast-paced flick. Be sure to check the minimum system requirements to make sure your PC can run the game.

Fast Times at Ridgemont High

Universal Pictures ★ Released 1982 ★ **Directed by** Amy Heckerling ★
Starring Sean Penn, Jennifer Jason Leigh, Judge Reinhold, Phoebe Cates, Brian Backer, Robert Romanus, Ray Walston

This humorous tale of sex, drugs, and rock 'n' roll—written by Cameron Crowe—takes a peek into the misadventures of California teenagers in the early '80s. Who could forget Sean Penn's performance as the ultimate surfer dude (and stoner), Spicoli?

From the main menu, select "Bonus Materials" and you'll see a long list of options. Forget about them for now—instead, press the Up Arrow on the remote, and the small white footprints will turn red. Press Enter to be treated to classic quotes from the film including "All I need are some tasty waves, cool buds, and I'm fine."

© 1982 Universal City Studios, Inc.

Even better—click on any of these quotes to launch its corresponding video clip from the film.

More of these "classic quotes" pages can be found on the main menu for the DVD (in the upper-right corner of the screen) and in the "Languages" section (footprints on the bottom right).

Fear and Loathing in Las Vegas

Universal Studios ★ Released 1998 ★ **Directed by** Terry Gilliam ★ **Starring** Johnny Depp, Benicio Del Toro

Based on the psychedelic book by Hunter S. Thompson, this film follows journalist Raoul Duke (Johnny Depp) and his friend and lawyer, Dr. Gonzo (Benicio Del Toro), on a writing assignment in Las Vegas. Problem is, they've consumed almost every illegal narcotic imaginable, resulting in a hallucinatory adventure they won't soon forget.

Film fanatics who enjoy watching movie trailers will certainly have fun uncovering these gems—especially since they're well hidden.

From the main menu, select "Bonus Materials" and then select "Cast & Filmmakers." Scroll down to "Directed by Terry Gilliam" and press Enter. You can read his bio by scrolling through the text using the Right Arrow. If you notice, the second-to-last page features a trailer to *12 Monkeys* (1995), and the last page of the bio has a trailer to *Brazil* (1985), both directed by Gilliam.

Fiddler on the Roof: Special Edition

MGM ★ Released 1971 ★ **Directed by** Norman Jewison ★ **Starring** Topol, Norma Crane, Leonard Frey, Molly Picon, Paul Mann

Based on the stories of Sholom Aleichem and the hit musical *Fiddler on the Roof,* this award-winning film takes place in early 20th century Russia as a Jewish peasant, Tevye (Topol), attempts to preserve tradition while marrying off his three daughters and coping with a changing political climate.

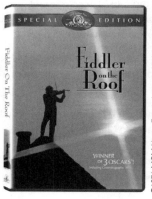

Pop in the "Special Features" side of the disc, and from the main menu, highlight the words "The Stories of Sholom Aleichem," but don't press Enter just yet. Instead, tap the Right Arrow on the DVD remote, and a small yellow silhouette of a fiddler sitting on a roof will appear. Press Enter and enjoy this short video of director Norman Jewison telling a story about a rich merchant and a beggar.

Allegedly, this story was heard during the original stage play of *Fiddler on the Roof*, but failed to make it into the film.

Field of Dreams: Collector's Edition

Universal Studios ★ Released 1989 ★ **Directed by** Phil Alden Robinson ★ **Starring** Kevin Costner, Amy Madigan, Ray Liotta, James Earl Jones, Burt Lancaster

"If you build it, he will come" is the classic line from this magical baseball movie.

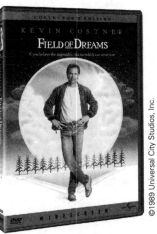

©1989 Universal City Studios, Inc.

Cash-strapped Iowa farmer Ray Kinsella (Kevin Costner) and his supportive wife Annie (Amy Madigan) decide to build a baseball diamond on their land, which is then visited by the ghosts of Shoeless Joe Jackson and several other Chicago White Sox players.

From the main menu, select "Bonus Materials" and the screen will offer five options. Select the first header ("The Field of Dreams Scrapbook"). Next, choose "Language Selection," and then "Spoken Language," and you'll see an option for "Musical Score."

Press Enter to watch the "Field of Dreams Scrapbook" documentary, but with only the soothing soundtrack in 5.1 surround sound.

Also, while it's not quite an egg, listen carefully on the "Bonus Materials" page, and you'll hear some dialogue from the film where Kevin Costner is told by a ghost to "Ease his pain."

Fight Club

20th Century Fox ★ Released 1999 ★ **Directed by** David Fincher ★ **Starring** Brad Pitt, Edward Norton, Helena Bonham Carter

Two unlikely associates begin an underground therapy group called the "Fight Club," and the concept catches on across America. A surprise twist near the end of the film had audiences buzzing, winning Brad Pitt and Edward Norton a nomination for "Best Action Team" at the 2000 Blockbuster Entertainment Awards.

Insert the second ("Supplemental") disc, and from the main menu, scroll across the bottom of the screen (using the Right Arrow) to select the "Advertising" tab. Once inside this new screen, press the Down Arrow a few times until a green smiley face appears in the lower-left corner of the screen. Now press Enter to view some of the official *Fight Club* merchandise such as soap bars, T-shirts, a golf shirt, backpack, clock, and more.

Be sure to read the entertaining descriptions for each of these products and how each ties into the film.

Another small egg can be found on the first disc. From the main menu, scroll across the bottom of the screen, and stop over the words "Special." Press the Up Arrow on the DVD remote, and another green smiley face will appear on the screen. Press Enter to view the production credits for this two-disc DVD set.

Did You Know?

Actors Brad Pitt and Edward Norton were intoxicated during the filming of the scene where they "play" drunk while practicing their golf swing. Allegedly, the balls were hitting the side of the catering truck!

Final Destination

New Line Cinema ★ Released 2000 **★ Directed** by James Wong **★ Starring**
Devon Sawa, Ali Larter, Kerr Smith, Tony Todd

"Death doesn't take no for an answer" is a fitting tagline for this underrated horror flick about a group of high-school friends en route to Paris. Something goes horribly wrong while they are flying on the plane, and the teenagers soon realize they cannot cheat death. Or can they?

Courtesy of New Line Home Entertainment, 2003.

Final Destination houses one of those Easter eggs where you don't even need to press anything in order to see it.

Each time the DVD is inserted into the player, the animated main menu will be different, with different characters from the film. This also happens whenever you head back to the main menu from other sections on the disc. These random menus also exist in other areas of the DVD, such as the "Special Features" screen and the "Audio Options" area. Cool!

There's another small egg—from the main menu, scroll down and select the white New Line logo in the bottom left-hand corner of the screen. Press Enter to scroll through four full pages of DVD and DVD-ROM credits. Now you know who to hire when you're creating your own DVDs!

Final Fantasy: The Spirits Within

Columbia Pictures ★ Released 2001 **★ Directed by** Hironobu Sakaguchi, Moto Sakakibara **★ Starring** Ming-Na, Alec Baldwin, Ving Rhames, Steve Buscemi, Peri Gilpin, Donald Sutherland, James Woods

In the year 2065 A.D., an evil alien presence is threatening humankind. The young Aki Ross is determined to save the planet by collecting eight spirits in the hopes of creating a force powerful enough to ward off the invaders. The movie, based on a popular Japanese video game series, features an all-computer-generated cast—but the "actors" look so lifelike!

There are seven good Easter eggs to be found on the DVDs. Pop in the first disc and from the main menu select "Special Features." Once inside, scroll down and select the last entry, "DVD-ROM Content," but don't press Enter yet. Instead, press the Up Arrow twice on the DVD remote and a white Japanese symbol will appear. Press Enter to see the female character Aki in a number of sexy outfits including a two-piece bathing suit and leather outfits. Wow, she looks real!

Most of the Easter eggs are on disc 2, so pop in that DVD now. From the main menu, enter the section entitled "Highlights Menu." Once inside, press the Up Arrow on the DVD remote and a symbol will illuminate at the bottom of the screen. Don't press Enter just yet—instead, press the Right Arrow and the symbol on the screen will become illuminated. Press Enter to access the second screen of bonus materials, and you'll see a new list of options. Now press the Up Arrow once and then the Right Arrow twice and the tiny video clip in the bottom right-hand corner of the screen will be highlighted. Press Enter to watch a lengthy music video parody of Michael Jackson's "Thriller"—featuring the computer-generated characters from *Final Fantasy: The Spirits Within*. Very clever, and very well done.

Now go back to the DVD's main menu and highlight the "Highlights Menu"— but don't press Enter this time. Instead, press the Right Arrow on the DVD remote and the cursor will disappear. Now press the Down Arrow and a blue and yellow symbol will appear on the screen. Press Enter to watch a compelling storyboard sequence of a romantic dinner between two of the main characters from the film. Nice piano music, too.

Now go back to the main menu and enter the "Highlights Menu" section. Then choose the "Vehicle Scale Comparisons" entry in the middle of the screen. Once inside, scroll down to highlight the arrow in the bottom left-hand corner of the screen. Press the Right Arrow twice and a blue symbol will appear on the screen. Press Enter to watch another entertaining slide show of colored sketches.

Now go back to the main menu and enter the "Highlights Menu" again, but this time enter the "Character Files" section. Scroll down and highlight the amber arrow. Press the Right Arrow and then the Left Arrow on the DVD remote. Another blue symbol will appear. Press Enter for another montage of sketches, all set to orchestrated music.

Wait—there's more!

From the main menu, select "Highlights Menu" and enter the second page of special features. Now select the "DVD-ROM Content" section (the last choice on the page). Once inside, highlight the arrow at the bottom of the screen and then press the Up Arrow on the DVD remote, followed by the Right Arrow. Now another blue and yellow symbol will appear on the screen. Press Enter for yet another storyboard sequence.

Finally, go back to the main menu again and highlight the words "Play Documentary" but don't press Enter just yet. Instead, press the Left Arrow on the DVD remote, followed by the Up Arrow. A blue Japanese symbol will appear on the screen. Press Enter to enjoy a 3-D rendering of Aki's head (with some lighting and color work reflecting off of it!).

Finding Forrester

Columbia Pictures ★ Released 2000 **★ Directed by** Gus Van Sant **★ Starring** Sean Connery, F. Murray Abraham, Anna Paquin, Busta Rymes, Rob Brown

From the director of *Good Will Hunting* comes this drama about a talented teenage basketball player (Rob Brown) whose secret passion is writing. Enter a reclusive Pulitzer Prize-winning novelist (Sean Connery), and their unlikely friendship forces them to re-evaluate their lives.

There are a couple of hidden pix on this disc if you know where to look. From the main menu, scroll down to the bottom and select the "Special Features" menu option. Once inside, choose "Filmographies" and then "Sean Connery." Now press the Up Arrow on the DVD remote and the movie title *The Untouchables* will illuminate. Press Enter to see a charming shot of Connery at the Oscars.

Now enter Anna Paquin's section and also press the Up Arrow on the DVD remote. *The Piano* will be highlighted. Press Enter to see a cute picture of a young Paquin holding her Oscar statuette.

Similarly, on the second page of F. Murray Abraham's filmography, press the Up Arrow and the movie *Amadeus* will be illuminated. Press Enter for Abraham's grinning face at the Oscars, holding his prize.

A Fish Called Wanda

MGM ★ **Released** 1988 ★ **Directed by** Charles Crichton ★ **Starring** John Cleese, Jamie Lee Curtis, Kevin Kline, Michael Palin

In this hilarious romantic comedy about thievery, trickery, and titillation, four unlikely jewelry store robbers band together to steal precious diamonds in London. But Wanda (Jamie Lee Curtis) and her boyfriend Otto (Kevin Kline) want the loot for themselves, so they call the cops on the ringleader, George (Tom Georgeson), who hides the diamonds in an unlikely place before he's arrested.

From this DVD's main menu, use the remote to navigate over to the treasure chest floating above the word "Languages." The lid of the chest will turn orange—press Enter and watch as the words and music fade, leaving nothing but this soothing aquarium screensaver!

To return to normal, press Enter again.

FM

Anchor Bay Entertainment ★ **Released** 1978 ★ **Directed by** John A. Alonzo ★ **Starring** Michael Brandon, Eileen Brennan, Alex Karras, Cleavon Little, Martin Mull, Cassie Yates

Los Angeles' most popular DJ, Jeff Dugan (Michael Brandon), and the wacky staff at QSKY will do anything to save the radio station from its money-hungry corporate officers who want to play more commercials and less rock 'n' roll.

The film includes performances by Tom Petty, REO Speedwagon, Jimmy Buffet, and Linda Ronstadt.

The egg on this DVD is quite easy to find—in fact, you don't have to do anything.

While almost all DVDs have a short, looped audio track that plays during the main menu, *FM* has an entire song if you let it play. Pop in the disc and from the main menu, turn up the volume and enjoy the entire "Tumbling Dice," performed by Rondstadt.

The Fog

MGM ★ **Released** 1979 ★ **Directed** by John Carpenter ★ **Starring** Adrienne Barbeau, Jamie Lee Curtis, John Houseman, Janet Leigh, Hal Holbrook

The centennial celebrations of the small town of Antonio Bay aren't going to go exactly as planned. As the thick fog rolls in, so does 100-year-old vengeance from ghostly seamen looking for bloody retribution.

As if all the extra features on this DVD weren't enough, MGM has crammed a few more on the disc. Pop in the DVD on the side that says "Widescreen/Special Features." From the main menu go to "Special Features" and press the Enter button on the DVD remote to access the section. Now press the Right Arrow button and a set of green eyes will appear in the top left-hand corner of the screen.

Press Enter to watch a montage of behind-the-scenes footage, including a host of special effects shots—all set to the film's creepy music.

And hey, you'll now be able to see how they made all that realistic fog!

For the Love of the Game

Universal Studios ★ **Released** 1999 ★ **Directed by** Sam Raimi ★ **Starring** Kevin Costner, Kelly Preston

Aging pitcher Billy Chapel (Kevin Costner) faces the end of his career just as his on-again off-again girlfriend Jane Aubrey (Kelly Preston) announces she's leaving him for a job in England. Much of the film takes place during Chapel's last game of the season, and through a series of flashbacks chronicling the ups and downs of his relationship with Aubrey.

While it's not quite an Easter egg since it's easily found on the disc, a trivia game on this DVD yields a special surprise for those who successfully answer all the questions.

From the main menu, scroll down and select the "On the Mound" baseball trivia game. If you get all 12 answers correct before you get three strikes, you'll hit a "Grand Slam." What does this mean? Sit back and enjoy a special 15-minute black-and-white short movie entitled *Slide, Babe, Slide*, a 1931 film about Babe Ruth.

Four of the Apocalypse

Anchor Bay Entertainment ★ Released 1975 **★ Directed by** Lucio Fulci ★
Starring Fabio Testi, Lynn Frederick, Michael J. Pollard, Harry Baird, Tomas Milian

Courtesy of Anchor Bay Entertainment ©2003.
©1975 mediatrade-Intramovies.

This ultra-violent spaghetti Western follows the gun-toting adventures of a gambler, a prostitute, a town drunk, and a madman—who all cross paths with a sadistic bandit. Now that's a recipe for a good Western!

The DVD for this little-known cult classic features an Easter egg, too. From the main menu, scroll over and select the "Extras" option. Once inside, press the Right Arrow four times until the sheriff's badge illuminates in red. Now press Enter and you'll be treated to a secret interview—it's a two-minute clip with actor Tomas "Chaco" Milian, who tells an amusing anecdote about working with horses as a child. (Warning: Foul language!)

Not for Prime Time: Four of the Apocalypse

What—you never heard of *Four of the Apocalypse*? Don't be surprised—due to its graphic violence, this film was banned in many countries, including the United States! Yup, this film was never released in American theaters but became available for home viewing for the first time on VHS. Ironically, fans of director Lucio Fulci—and Lucio himself—consider this 104-minute film to be his best work.

Fried Green Tomatoes: Collector's Edition

Universal Studios ★ Released 1991 **★ Directed by** Jon Avnet **★ Starring**
Kathy Bates, Jessica Tandy, Mary Stuart Masterson, Mary-Louise Parker

This heartwarming "chick flick" takes place in a small Georgia town, Whistle Stop, where unhappily married Evelyn Couch (Kathy Bates) visits a nursing home and listens to an inspiring story spun by the elder Ninny Threadgoode (Jessica Tandy).

©1991 Fried Green Tomatoes Productions

Common in many Universal DVD movies is a hidden musical score, but this one can be a little tricky to find. Here's how to do it:

From the main menu, select "Bonus Materials" and then select the documentary, "Moments of Discovery: The Making of Fried Green Tomatoes." Now, instead of selecting "Play," scroll down and select "Language." On the left of the screen, you'll see "Musical Score." Tap the Left Arrow on the remote, and the words "Musical Score" will be highlighted with red borders. Press Enter to watch the documentary—but with only the classical music score playing in the background.

Friends: The Complete First Season

Warner Bros. ★ Series Began 1994 **★ Starring** Jennifer Aniston, Courteney Cox, Lisa Kudrow, Matt LeBlanc, Matthew Perry, David Schwimmer

This complete season-one box set of *Friends*—one of the most successful TV sitcoms in history—features four DVDs packed with more than 20 episodes, special features, and an Easter egg, too.

Insert the fourth disc from this set, and select "Special Features" from the main menu. Now press Enter to select the first of these features, "Friends of Friends." This page is a guestbook of celebrities—such as Jay Leno, Helen Hunt, and George Clooney—who have appeared on the show. Selecting any of these will launch a video clip with their appearances.

This isn't the egg, of course, but if you press the Left Arrow from this "Friends of Friends" screen, you'll notice that the steaming coffee cup in the upper-left corner of the screen will now have a blue circle around it. Press Enter to watch a casting call take place during a show (where Joey [Matt LeBlanc] was trying out for a part); little does the audience know that the three "casting directors" are none other than *Friends*' executive producers Kevin Bright, Martha Kauffman, and David Crane.

Fright

Anchor Bay Entertainment ★ **Released** 1971 ★ **Directed by** Peter Collinson ★ **Starring** Honor Blackman, Susan George, Ian Bannen, John Gregson

Courtesy of Anchor Bay Entertainment ©2003.
©1971 Fantale Films Ltd.

When a teenage girl baby-sits for the Lloyd family's youngest son, a number of strange occurrences take place in the creepy house. However, the young Helen is in for even more "fright" when the child's biological father appears after escaping from a psychiatric institution. Don't you hate it when that happens?

From the main menu, select "Extras" from the list of options (it's in the middle). You'll notice that the cursor is a knife that turns bloody when you press Enter. Cool! NO, that's not the Easter egg. Once inside, press the Right Arrow on the DVD remote and one of Ian Bannen's eyes will turn blue. Now press Enter to watch a hidden two-minute interview clip with the film's star, Honor Blackman.

From Hell

20th Century Fox ★ **Released** 2001 ★ **Directed by** Albert Hughes, Allen Hughes ★ **Starring** Johnny Depp, Heather Graham

From Hell embarks on a chilling journey of bloodlust, back when Jack the Ripper terrorized the streets of London at the turn of the 20th century. Johnny Depp plays a drug-addicted clairvoyant detective, Fred Abberline, who with a homeless prostitute, Mary Kelly (Heather Graham), is determined to catch Jack the Ripper in the act.

From the main menu of the second DVD, scroll down and highlight the words "Absinthe Makes The Heart Grow Fonder," but don't press Enter. Instead, press the

Down Arrow and then the Right Arrow, and the scalpel in the travel kit will illuminate in white. Press Enter to watch a 40-minute UK film, *Jack The Ripper: The Final Solution,* based on Stephen Knight's classic book.

Now switch discs and pop in the first DVD.

From the main menu, select "Language Selection" and then scroll down to the bottom of the screen until the words "Main Menu" are highlighted. Instead of pressing Enter, press the Right Arrow on the DVD remote, and the eye will open. Now press Enter to view the DVD credits.

Go back to the main menu and select "Special Features." Press the number 5 on the remote, and a yellow silhouette of Jack the Ripper will appear, followed by a THX demonstration.

Futurama: Volume One

20th Century Fox ★ Series Began 1999 **★ Developed by** Matt Groening, David X. Cohen **★ Starring** Billy West, Katey Sagal, John Di Maggio, Lauren Tom, Phil LaMarr

From Matt Groening, the creator of *The Simpsons*, comes his latest masterpiece: *Futurama*. This clever animated TV series follows the antics of Fry, a pizza delivery guy, who is accidentally zapped to the 30th century.

Have this season one collection? Have the time? Good, because there are plenty of eggs to unlock. Here we go….

Pop in the first disc. From the main menu, scroll down to highlight the words "Love Labours Lost in Space" but don't press Enter. Instead, tap the Right Arrow and the flying car will turn yellow. Now press Enter to see a fake movie poster spoofing *Planet of the Apes*.

Now insert the second DVD into your player. From the main menu, scroll down and highlight the episode "Hell Is Other Robots" but don't press Enter. Instead, press the Down Arrow once and the flying Slurm truck will illuminate. Now press Enter to see yet another fake movie poster.

From the main menu of the second disc, enter the episode entitled "Fear of a Bot Planet" (the first option on the screen). Once inside, choose "Scene Selection" (third from the top) and then highlight the fourth window (with Bender shaking his fist). Instead of pressing Enter, press the Left Arrow on the DVD remote and the "NNY" button will illuminate. Press Enter for another cute movie poster parody.

Now go back to the main menu and select the "My Three Suns" episode. Once inside, enter the "Scene Selection" section. Now scroll down to the bottom and highlight the words "Main Menu" but don't press Enter. Instead, press the Left Arrow and the three yellow buttons (on the console) will turn red. Press Enter for another movie poster.

Now go back to the main menu and select the episode "Hell Is Other Robots," and once again enter the "Scene Selection" area. Once inside, highlight Scene 3 (with Bender at the computer). Press the Right Arrow and the squiggly symbol will light up. Press Enter for yet another movie poster.

Now pop in the third and final disc. From the main menu, scroll down and highlight the episode entitled "Fry and the Slurm Factory" (the last option) but don't press Enter. Instead, press the Down Arrow once and the police car in the corner will illuminate. Now press Enter for—you guessed it—another clever movie poster parody (this time of *Buffy the Vampire Slayer!*).

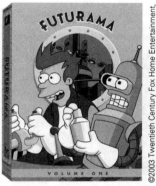

Go back to the main menu and now enter the episode entitled "A Flight to Remember" (the first option) and then enter the "Scene Selection" area again. Scroll over to highlight Scene 4 but don't press Enter. Instead, press the Left Arrow on the DVD remote and the "Do Not Push" button will light up. Press Enter now to see the professor in his birthday suit! Er, thankfully, a pink ribbon covers his privates!

Tired yet? Wait—there's still more!

From the main menu, select any of the four episodes and enter the "Special Features" section. Scroll down to highlight the words "Main Menu," but press the Right Arrow instead of Enter to highlight the remote on the right-hand side of the screen. Now press Enter to see another movie poster parody—this time for *Star Wars*. And yes, it's the same poster for each episode.

And finally, once inside any of the four different "Special Features" menus, enter the "Image Gallery" section and start scrolling through the sketches. Once in a while you'll see a colored spaceship in the corner. Press Enter when you see one of these to launch a corresponding video clip. There are four different ones to find, each narrated by the series' creator extraordinaire, Matt Groening.

Galaxy Quest

DreamWorks Pictures ★ **Released** 1999 ★ **Directed by** Dean Parisot ★
Starring Tim Allen, Sigourney Weaver, Alan Rickman, Tony Shalhoub, Sam Rockwell, Daryl Mitchell

In this funny *Star Trek* knock-off, the retired cast of a sci-fi TV show is beamed aboard a real spaceship by desperate aliens to help save the universe.

Er, Tim Allen is in charge of our fate? Lord help us!

Here's how to access the space-age Easter eggs on this disc. From the main menu, you'll see that the last entry is entitled "Omega 13." If you scroll down and select it, you'll see that you can't access it. Why? Because you need to see the movie first, silly. So go ahead and do that—or select "Scene Index" and choose the last scene (Number 20, a.k.a. "End Credits"). Now go back to the main menu, select "Omega 13," and enjoy this short animated clip.

Courtesy of DreamWorks Home Entertainment.

There are a handful of other small Easter eggs scattered throughout this disc. From the main menu, select "Special Features" and then choose the "Cast and Crew" option near the bottom of the page. Once inside, enter the biographies for actors Tim Allen, Sigourney Weaver, Alan Rickman, Tony Shalhoub, Daryl Mitchell, and Sam Rockwell, and crew members Dean Parisot, Mark Johnson, Charles Newirth, and Stan Winston. Here's what to do—once inside each biography, press the Up Arrow on the first page and a little film reel at the top of the page will become illuminated. Press Enter to watch some corresponding interview clips. Great fun!

Gladiator

DreamWorks Pictures ★ **Released** 2000 ★ **Directed by** Ridley Scott ★
Starring Russell Crowe

In this Academy Award-winning feature film, Roman general Maximus (Russell Crowe) seeks revenge for the murder of his family. Now a slave, his only way to get back to Rome to face his nemesis—the corrupt Emperor Commodus (Joaquin Phoenix)—is to become a gladiator.

There are two good Easter eggs on this critically acclaimed action epic.

Insert the second disc and scroll down to select the word "More." Now visit the "Trailers and TV Spots" area. Ignore all of these options, and press the Left Arrow on the remote; the amulet around the neck of Emperor Marcus Aurelius (Richard Harris) will turn red. Press Enter and enjoy a hilarious *Chicken Run* trailer modeled after the dramatic *Gladiator* theme ("An egg that became a chicken, a chicken that became a leader!" and so forth). Great fun.

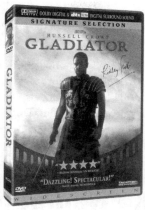

Another egg can be found on this second disc by going to "Original Storyboards." Click on the "More" tab and choose "Rhino Fight." Press the Up Arrow and the rhino in the middle of the screen will turn gray. Press Enter to read about a deleted scene featuring a rhinoceros, view the related script and storyboard sequence, and even watch test footage of a digitally created rhino.

Glengarry Glen Ross: Special Edition

New Line Cinema/Artisan ★ **Released** 1992 ★ **Directed by** James Foley ★ **Starring** Al Pacino, Jack Lemmon, Alec Baldwin, Ed Harris, Alan Arkin, Kevin Spacey

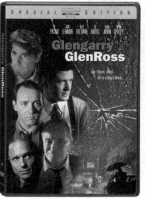

Hollywood's adaptation of David Mamet's play is a sobering tale of what desperate men can do in desperate situations. This drama chronicles the life of a handful of shysters in a boiler room under pressure to perform. Every performance is, in a word, brilliant.

And so is the Easter egg.

Pop in the second disc (the "Full Screen" version of the film), and from the main menu scroll to the bottom and select "Special Features." Now scroll down all the way to the bottom and highlight the words "Main Menu," but don't press Enter. Instead, press the Left Arrow on the DVD remote and the word "BAR" will illuminate in the window on the left. Press Enter.

It says, "Blake's monologue from the film *Glengarry Glen Ross* is one of the most popular scenes for actors to perform in auditions." Keep watching and you'll see a handful of drama students—male and female, young and old—delivering the classic lines from the film. This clip is about seven minutes in length.

Great idea for an egg!

The Godfather—DVD Collection

Paramount Pictures ★ Released 1972 (*The Godfather*), 1974 (*The Godfather: Part II*), 1990 (*The Godfather: Part III*) ★ **Directed by** Francis Ford Coppola ★ **Starring** Marlon Brando, Al Pacino, Diane Keaton, Robert De Niro, Richard S. Castellano, Robert Duvall, James Caan, John Cazale, Andy Garcia

This five-disc trilogy chronicles the infamous lives of the Corleone mob family through multiple generations.

There are a few good eggs buried deep inside this collection, and all of them can be found on the fourth disc, "Bonus Materials."

From the main menu, select the "SetUp" section, and then tap the Right Arrow on the DVD remote. A globe will appear on the screen. Press Enter and enjoy this humorous collage of famous *Godfather* scenes—but in multiple languages as seen throughout the world. Ever wanted to know what "Ba-da-boom" sounds like in German?

A second egg can be found in the "Galleries" section of the disc. Scroll down to "DVD Credits" and press Enter. Now click "Next" four times to be treated to a hidden clip from the show *The Sopranos* as Tony and company attempt to watch a bootleg version of *The Godfather* on DVD!

There's more…

From the main menu, select the option "The Family Tree." Now use the DVD remote to navigate around and select "Santino ('Sonny')." Press Enter again to launch Sonny Corleone's biography. Press the Left Arrow and James Caan's picture will turn white. Press Enter to read Caan's biography. Press the Left Arrow again, and this new picture of him will also turn white. Press Enter—now you can watch his screen tests as Sonny Corleone.

Lastly, from the main menu, select the word "Filmmakers" and once inside, enter the Mario Puzo biography. Press the Left Arrow twice, and a large, green dollar sign will fill the screen. Press Enter to view a humorous conversation between Francis Ford Coppola and Mario Puzo as they play pool. Coppola asks Puzo why he wrote the book *The Godfather*. His answer? "To make money!"

Gremlins 2: The New Batch

Warner Bros. ★ Released 1990 **★ Directed by** Joe Dante **★ Starring** Zach Galligan, Phoebe Cates, John Glover, Robert Prosky, Robert Picardo, Christopher Lee

"Here they grow again" was the tagline for this sci-fi/comedy sequel. Once again, Gizmo the Mogwai must band together with his human owners to face off against a new breed of nasty Gremlins. This time around, the mean, green, reproducing machines have taken over a New York skyscraper.

There is a monstrous Easter egg on this disc, too. From the main menu, scroll down twice and select "Special Features." Now highlight the words "Gag Reel" near the bottom of the screen but don't press Enter. Instead, tap the Right Arrow on the DVD remote and the green claw will turn purple. Press Enter to watch an alternate home video sequence, with some fun Gremlin antics, movie parodies, and cartoon clips. Great fun!

Hackers

MGM ★ Released 1995 ★ **Directed by** Iain Softley ★ **Starring** Jonny Lee Miller, Angelina Jolie, Fisher Stevens, Lorraine Bracco

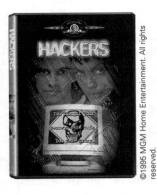

In this film set during the dawn of the Information Age, a young computer genius and his pals pull off a near-impossible task of hacking into a highly secured computer at the Ellington Mineral Corporation. But in doing so, they stumble upon a high-tech embezzling scheme masked by a computer virus.

Hackers was also the film to put Angelina Jolie on the map.

Looking to hack into the DVD to find its egg? No need—here's how to locate it:

From the main menu, press the Left Arrow on the remote, and the logo for *Hackers* will illuminate in beige.

Press Enter on the remote, and this will take you to a screen where you're asked to input the proper password from the list of options: Sex, Secret, Love, or God.

Use the remote to navigate over the word "God," press Enter, and the words "Access Granted" will flash on the screen. Following this will be a short computer-generated sequence of soaring through the insides of a computer.

Halloween

Anchor Bay Entertainment ★ Released 1978 ★ **Directed by** John Carpenter ★ **Starring** Donald Pleasence, Jamie Lee Curtis, P.J. Soles, Nancy Loomis

The quintessential '70s horror flick, John Carpenter's *Halloween* stars Donald Pleasence as a disturbed Michael Meyers, who goes on a murderous rampage after breaking out of a mental hospital. And you just gotta love that creepy *Halloween* theme music!

Pop in this disc and choose the widescreen version of the film. At the very ending of the film, after the credits roll and the screen fades to black, wait about ten seconds and a photo of Laurie

Strode (Jamie Lee Curtis) in the kitchen will appear, with Michael Meyers in the window. This photo was doctored to advertise the DVD production company. See their logo? Clever and creepy.... (Note: This will work only with the regular version of the film, not the "Extended Edition" DVD rerelease.)

Hannibal

MGM ★ Released 2001 ★ **Directed by** Ridley Scott ★ **Starring** Anthony Hopkins, Julianne Moore

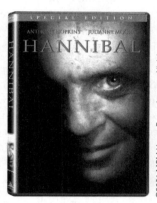

Dr. Hannibal Lecter (Anthony Hopkins) is back in this creepy sequel to *Silence of the Lambs.* The intelligent, perverse, and manipulative killer lures FBI agent Clarice Starling (Julianne Moore) into a deadly game of survival and suspense.

Insert the "Special Features" DVD (disc 2) and from the main menu, select the first option: "Breaking the Silence, The Making of Hannibal."

Now scroll down and place the cursor over the "Music" option, but don't press Enter. Instead, press the Left Arrow on the DVD remote, and the two little up arrows will change to blue. Now press Enter to watch a few minutes of Clarice's "Flashframes," the brief bursts of film exposed from the time a director yells "Cut!" to the moment the camera is turned off.

Another point of interest: *Hannibal* music editor Mark Streitenfeld wrote, performed, and produced an original song entitled "Clarice" specifically for this unusual montage.

Did You Know?

There are some fun continuity errors to try and catch in *Harry Potter and the Sorcerer's Stone*. Here are a couple of them:

On the train to Hogwarts, Ron Weasley's hair is parted in different places throughout the ride. You'll see it go from a part in the middle to no part at all once he asks Harry about his scar!

After arriving at Hogwarts, Harry takes a seat opposite Hermione Granger, but in the following cut (when the feast begins), he's right beside her! Now that's magic!

Harry Potter and the Sorcerer's Stone

Warner Bros. ★ **Released** 2001 ★ **Directed by** Chris Columbus ★ **Starring** Daniel Radcliffe, Rupert Grint, Emma Watson

One of the most successful contemporary book series for kids (aged 7 to 77) makes its way onto the silver screen. *Harry Potter and the Sorcerer's Stone* tells the tale of young Harry Potter as he attends the Hogwarts School of Witchcraft and Wizardry.

From the main menu, press the Right Arrow on the DVD remote, and the owl will have some magic sparkles around it. Press Enter to read that you've been accepted at Hogwarts School of Witchcraft and Wizardry. You'll also be instructed to insert disc 2.

From the main menu of the second disc, choose "Diagon Alley" and you'll be told to choose the bricks in the correct sequence in order to enter the alley. The solution is to work counterclockwise. On the DVD remote, press the Left Arrow, Up Arrow, Up Arrow again, and then press Enter. Next press the Up Arrow and then Enter. Now it's Up Arrow and then Enter again. Now tap the Right Arrow, Down Arrow, Down Arrow again, and Enter. Lastly, it's Down Arrow and then Enter. This will give you access. Don't worry—if you mess up, the bricks will move and you'll be let in soon enough.

Now you'll be inside the alleyway (as in the film!). Before you purchase a wand, you'll need money, so access the "Gringotts" bank. When you navigate to the Gringotts sign, press the Down Arrow, and the key will be highlighted. Now press Enter to get inside the bank.

Once inside, press the Down Arrow and the jellybeans will be highlighted. Press Enter for a close-up of "Every Flavour Beans." Click around the screen with the DVD remote to read about a few of the flavors offered.

OK, down to business:

While at the bank, tap the Right Arrow and then Enter to open your vault. Take a look at that stash of gold and silver! Listen to the instructions for a clue on what to do next. Exit to the alley and then enter "Ollivanders" wand store. It doesn't matter which wand you choose by navigating around the shelves with the DVD remote—after a few wrong (and explosive!) picks, the right one will be handed to you.

Once you have your wand, it's time for class. Head back to the main menu, and select "Classrooms" from the middle of the screen. Here, select "Potions" and once inside this new screen, press the Right Arrow to highlight the mortar and pestle.

Press Enter. Now choose the right ingredients to make each of the three potions and then mix them. "But do be careful," warns your narrator.

First, choose to create a sleeping potion. Do this by selecting "Wormwood" and "Asphodel" (by pressing Enter over both vials). Now you're asked what another name is for "Aconite." The correct answer is "Monkshood" and "Wolfsbane," so select these from the vials by pressing Enter on both. Next, you're asked what you need to cure a boil! The answer, of course, is "Porcupine Quills" and "Snake Fangs." Press Enter on both of these ingredients to pass this stage of the game.

Now you must look for a key (among many flying keys). The correct one can be chosen by pressing the following on the DVD remote: Right Arrow, Up Arrow, Up Arrow again, Right Arrow, and then Enter. It'll be the small key in the back.

If you've kept up this far, good for you! But your work is still not done yet. Take a look at this screen and you must now select from one of the seven bottles available here—within 60 seconds. The answer is the yellow round one in the middle. Scroll over to it and press Enter.

And here's the payoff—you'll be taken to the magic mirror and handed the sorcerer's stone. Press the Up Arrow and then Enter to take it. Congratulations—you will be transported through the mirror to a secret screen with seven fantastic bonus videos, including many deleted scenes from the film.

(Note: There are other ways to access this Sorcerer's Stone, which will unlock the extra goodies. The above scenario is but one! Enjoy trying to find other ways to access this hidden material.)

Highlander 4: Endgame

Dimension Films ★ Released 2000 ★ **Directed by** Douglas Aarniokoski ★ **Starring** Adrian Paul, Christopher Lambert

To combat a ruthless and relentless band of immortals, Connor Macleod (Christopher Lambert) and his brother Duncan (Adrian Paul) team up to battle the forces of darkness. Remember, in the end, there can be only one!

From the main menu of the first disc, press the Left Arrow, and a yellow insignia will appear. Press Enter and the screen will explain that this is just one of six "Watcher Files" planted on this disc. You'll need to find the other five to beat Jacob Kell in the "There can be only one" trivia game on this disc.

The first hint, for example, is that Connor Macleod was an early pioneer in the orange juice business, but he later found the antique business better suited to his lifestyle.

Some of these Watcher Files contain video clips, too.

The second and third Watcher symbols can be found in the "Bonus Materials" menu by pressing the Left Arrow in the "Feature Audio Commentary" section, and in the "Deleted Scenes" section on the second page of "Bonus Materials."

The last three symbols are in the "Captions" section, the "Sneak Peeks" section, and the "DVD-ROM" section—all from the main menu. For each of these three symbols, press the Left Arrow and then press Enter.

Mel Brooks' History of the World: Part 1

20th Century Fox ★ Released 1981 **★ Directed by** Mel Brooks **★ Starring** Mel Brooks, Dom DeLuise, Madeline Kahn, Harvey Korman, Cloris Leachman, Ron Carey, Gregory Hines, Pamela Stephenson, Andreas Voutsinas, Shecky Green, Sid Ceasar

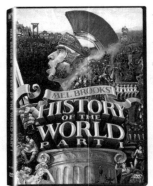

Take a hilarious ride through history— from the dawn of man, through the Spanish Inquisition, to the Space Age—as seen through the eyes of Mel Brooks.

And hey, there's an Easter egg on this wacky DVD, too. From the main menu, select any of the options, such as "Language Selection," "Scene Selection," or "Theatrical Trailer." Now go back to the main menu and you'll notice that the interface has changed! You can keep doing this to see different graphics, actors, and other funny references from the film—including one with dead rats. How lovely.

©2003 Twentieth Century Fox Home Entertainment, Inc.

Galaxy Quest

Though it's not quite an Easter egg, a funny mistake appears on the DVD for *Galaxy Quest* (pae 66). In the "Cast and Crew" filmography/ biography section (inside the "Special Features" area), there's a listing for actor "Brandon Long." Problem is, his name is Justin Long—Brandon is the name of the character Justin played in this film! Whoops!

How High

Universal Pictures ★ **Released** 2001 ★ **Directed by** Jesse Dylan ★
Starring Method Man, Redman

Consider this movie as hip-hop meets Cheech & Chong. Two unlikely Harvard students (played by rappers Method Man and Redman) shake things up a little at the Ivy League school with their penchant for partying.

There's a little Easter egg hunt to try on the DVD, with some help from Method Man and Redman.

From the main menu, enter the "Bonus Materials" page, and scroll down to highlight the words "Hide the Stash." Press the Right Arrow. A red cigarette lighter will appear on the chalkboard. Press Enter to watch a humorous clip of "Pimpology 101."

Go to the second page of "Bonus Materials." Highlight the words "Music Videos," and then press the Left Arrow, and the number *420* will turn red at the top of the screen. Press Enter.

"Sorry bro," they'll tell you. This isn't it.

Now, while still on the second page of "Bonus Materials," scroll down and highlight the words "Universal Showcase." Now press the Right Arrow, and the number *420* will turn red at the bottom of the screen. Press Enter.

"That's not it—you're too cold!"

Click "More" to be taken to the third and final page of "Bonus Materials," scroll down to highlight the arrow beside the word "Back," and then press the Up Arrow. The number *420* will turn red. Press Enter.

"Damn, use your brain!" they yell.

Now scroll down to highlight the words "DVD Newsletter" and press the Right Arrow; the number *420* will turn red between the two girls on the right. Press Enter.

"Whoa! You finally found it, huh? It only took you about, what, 48 days?"

How to Clean Your DVDs

It's happened to all of us—you're trying to watch a DVD, but the disc is "stuttering" worse than Ken in *A Fish Called Wanda*. What to do? You could purchase one of those cleaning kits at your local retailer, or you can try the cheaper home remedy—and it works. Take a cotton cloth or any smooth towel (note: do not use tissues), and find some rubbing alcohol (even cheap perfume will do). While holding the DVD by its outer rim, spray a *bit* of the liquid onto the underside of the disc (the part the laser reads), and gently wipe in an outward motion from the inside out and not in circles. Be sure to wait until it dries before putting it back into the player. Chances are, you've removed most or all of the dirt from the grooves.

Independence Day

20th Century Fox ★ **Released** 1996 ★ **Directed by** Roland Emmerich ★
Starring Will Smith, Bill Pullman, Jeff Goldblum

In one of the biggest sci-fi flicks in Hollywood history, the fate of the human race is at stake as Earth is invaded by war-hungry aliens in huge spaceships. A band of survivors vows to fight back, including Capt. Steven "Eagle" Hiller (Will Smith), U.S. President Thomas J. Whitmore (Bill Pullman), and ex-scientist David Levinson (Jeff Goldblum).

The two-disc "Five Star Collection" DVD features two versions of the film and a slew of bonus materials.

Pop in the second DVD, and from the main menu, select "Data Console" in the bottom-right corner of the screen. Once inside, highlight the words "Main Menu," but don't press Enter—tap the Right Arrow instead, and a little red light will appear on the personal computer. Press Enter and the disc will be inserted into the PC. "Systems Activated—Access 7-4-Enter" will flash on the screen. Also notice that the spaceship is floating in the background.

"Access 7-4-Enter" is a clue on what to do next.

Click on "Main Menu" and you'll see the ship is hovering. You only have seven seconds to punch in the password, which is 7, 4, and then Enter. Having done this, you'll now be inside the spacecraft. On some DVD players, you'll need to press the 10+ button seven times, followed by the 4, and then Enter. Experiment to get it right—because the payoff is worth it. (Remember, Independence Day is July 4th—hence the 7 and 4.)

This new menu screen inside the ship offers a handful of hidden features including isolated audio tracks, explosion scenes from the movie, fake news broadcasts created for the film, extended sequences, DVD credits, and more.

Jacob's Ladder: Special Edition

Artisan ★ Released 1990 **★ Directed by** Adrian Lyne **★ Starring** Tim Robbins

This psychological horror film follows the dissolution of a dying Vietnam vet, Jacob Singer (played by Tim Robbins). Singer and the audience are taken on a twisted and terrifying journey where it becomes difficult to tell what's real.

Courtesy of Artisan Home Entertainment Inc.

Though not specified on the DVD box, a handful of extras are stored on the *Jacob's Ladder* "Special Edition" DVD. They include numerous deleted scenes, deleted scenes with commentary, full-length audio commentary for the entire film, a promotional TV spot, and a 26-minute "making-of" documentary entitled "Building Jacob's Ladder."

Although these features are not exactly hidden, they are indeed unadvertised and undocumented features worth mentioning (and viewing!).

Jay and Silent Bob
Strike Back

Dimension Films/Buena Vista Pictures ★ **Released** 2000 ★ **Directed by** Kevin Smith ★ **Starring** Ben Affleck, Eliza Dushku, Shannon Elizabeth, Will Ferrell, Ali Larter, Jason Lee, Jason Mewes, Kevin Smith, Chris Rock

Jay (Jason Mewes) and Silent Bob (Kevin Smith), two buds from past Kevin Smith films such as *Clerks, Mallrats, Chasing Amy,* and *Dogma,* head out on a cross-country road trip from New Jersey to Hollywood. It seems a major motion picture is being based on their likeness, and they want to get the cash they deserve.

If you want to see Mewes' privates (no kidding), then you may want to unlock this DVD Easter egg. But you've been forewarned....

Insert the second disc and then click "More" to go to the second page of special features. Now select "Cast and Crew Filmographies," and then choose "Jason Mewes—Jay." Once inside, press the Up Arrow on the DVD remote until the word "Balls" appears at the top of the screen in red.

Now press Enter to see Mewes pull down his pants (facing away from the camera), exposing his, er, manhood. (Warning: Nudity.)

Jerry Maguire: Special Edition

TriStar Pictures ★ **Released** 1996 ★ **Directed by** Cameron Crowe ★ **Starring** Tom Cruise, Cuba Gooding Jr., Renee Zellweger, Kelly Preston, Jerry O'Connell, Jay Mohr, Bonnie Hunt, Regina King

Tom Cruise plays Jerry Maguire, a ruthless sports agent who had it all—but when his professional and personal life begin to crumble, Maguire must re-evaluate his scruples while trying to woo a single mom and make a star out of an up-and-coming athlete.

"Show me the Easter eggs!" Sorry—couldn't resist. Pop in disc 2 and from the main menu select "Special Features." Once inside, choose "Director and Cast Video Commentary." Now navigate over to the words "Mission Statement" (the "#2" entry on the page) but don't press Enter. Instead, press the Right Arrow on the DVD remote and then press the Up Arrow. A number of dates on the calendar will be filled in. Now press Enter to watch over five minutes of backstage antics with Tom Cruise and co. while working on the video commentary for the DVD.

It can be a bit tricky to do this, so here's a shortcut: During the movie itself simply press the Title button on your DVD remote and then press 1 and 6 (or 10+ and 6) on the DVD remote.

Joe Somebody

20th Century Fox ★ Released 2001 **★ Directed by** John Pasquin **★ Starring** Tim Allen, Julie Bowen, Kelly Lynch, Greg Germann, Hayden Panettiere, Jim Belushi

Joe Scheffer is an overworked and underappreciated office jockey (played by Tim Allen) who decides to fight back after being humiliated in front of his daughter on "Bring Your Kid to Work Day." This family comedy follows Scheffer's makeover and martial arts training as he gains strength, confidence, and respect.

©2003 Twentieth Century Fox Home Entertainment, Inc.

Want an egg? Of course you do! From the main menu, enter the section entitled "Scene Selections." Once inside, choose Scenes 13 through 16 and then highlight Scene 13, without pressing Enter just yet. Instead, press the Up Arrow on the DVD remote and Tim Allen's arm will turn into a bulging yellow bicep. Press Enter and it'll turn red before revealing the Easter egg—a deleted scene with optional commentary by director John Pasquin. This steamy scene is entitled "Callie Visits Joe at Night."

Jerry Maguire: Tidbits

- Ethan Valhere is the name of the character played by actor Eric Stoltz. Interestingly, Valhere is also the name of Stoltz's character in 1989's *Say Anything*—also directed by Cameron Crowe!
- Jann Wenner, who plays "Scully" in this film, is the publisher of *Rolling Stone* magazine. Writer/director Cameron Crowe once worked at *Rolling Stone—as chronicled in his film Almost Famous.*
- The title role, played by Tom Cruise, was originally written for another Tom—Tom Hanks.

Joy Ride

20th Century Fox ★ Released 2001 **★ Directed by** John Dahl **★ Starring** Paul Walker, Steve Zahn, Leelee Sobieski

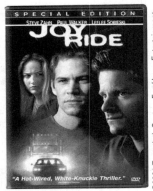

On this nail-biting thrill-ride, brothers Lewis and Fuller Thomas (Paul Walker and Steve Zahn) play a prank on a lonely truck driver who doesn't take the joke too well. Their cross-country drive with Lewis' college friend Venna Wilcox (Leelee Sobieski) becomes a deadly flight for their lives from the vengeful trucker who won't give up the chase until the boys have been taught a lesson.

From the disc's main menu, select the "Extra Features" menu at the bottom of the screen, and then select "Deleted Scene and Alternate Endings."

Now press the Up Arrow, and the car's taillights will turn red. Press Enter to read the DVD production credits.

And while they're not an egg, be sure to view the four alternate endings to this suspenseful film. What a treat!

Jurassic Park III: Collector's Edition

Universal Pictures ★ Released 2001 **★ Directed by** Joe Johnston **★ Starring** Sam Neill, William H. Macy, Téa Leoni

Renowned paleontologist Dr. Alan Grant (Sam Neill) agrees to accompany wealthy adventurer Paul Kirby (William H. Macy) and his wife, Amanda (Téa Leoni), on an aerial tour of Isla Sorna, InGen's former breeding ground for dinosaurs. The plane crashes onto the island, and the gang must (once again) outrun and outsmart the prehistoric beasts.

While not quite a dinosaur-sized Easter egg, there's an interesting undocumented extra planted on this "Collector's Edition" DVD.

From the main menu, scroll down to the second option, and select "Bonus Materials." Now click to the second page and select "Jurassic Park III Archives." The "Poster Gallery" inside, once selected, will display a slide show of 20 or so *Jurassic Park III* posters for the film.

These "Jurassic Park III Archives" also provide a montage of photos from the film that scroll by with the movie's theme music playing in the background.

Kiss of the Dragon

20th Century Fox ★ Released 2001 **★ Directed by** Chris Nahon **★ Starring** Jet Li, Bridget Fonda

Wrapped up in a deadly conspiracy and falsely accused of murder, China's top intelligence agent Liu Jian (Jet Li) is on the run in Paris with the help of a seductive call girl, Jessica (Bridget Fonda), whose daughter is locked away in an orphanage.

The DVD of this martial arts thriller features a handful of extras including commentaries, featurettes, trailers, and of course, an Easter egg.

From the main menu, scroll across to the right, and press Enter over the "Special Features" tab. Once inside, click down to "Police Gymnasium Fight: Martial Arts Demo" and press Enter. Now scroll down and highlight the words "Demo Two," but instead of pressing Enter, press the Right Arrow on the DVD remote, and a silver dragon will appear on Jet Li's black shirt.

Press Enter to view an alternate, extended trailer for *Kiss of the Dragon*.

K-PAX

Universal Pictures ★ Released 2001 **★ Directed by** Iain Softley **★ Starring** Kevin Spacey, Jeff Bridges, Alfre Woodard, Mary McCormack

This critically acclaimed sci-fi drama follows a stranger who calls himself Prot (Kevin Spacey), who claims to be from the planet K-PAX. Jeff Bridges plays Dr. Mark Powell, whose doubts and disbelief turn to amazement as he learns more about Prot's abilities. But is he really an alien? You'll have to watch the film to find out (and you still may never know!).

Dig movie trailers? Then you'll love the Easter eggs hidden on *K-Pax*. Pop in the disc, and from the main menu select "Bonus Materials." Select the word "More" twice, until you land on the third page of extras for this film. The second option on this screen will read "Now Showing." Press Enter to view trailers for these films: *Apollo 13*, *The Family Man*, *Notting Hill*, *Meet Joe Black*, and *Patch Adams*. After the montage is finished, you can highlight the film reel for each DVD to watch the theatrical trailer. Enjoy!

©2003 Universal Studios Home Video.

Kung Pow: Enter the Fist

20th Century Fox ★ **Released** 2002 ★ **Directed by** Steve Oedekerk ★ **Starring** Steve Oedekerk, Jennifer Tung, Leo Lee

©2003 Twentieth Century Fox Home Entertainment, Inc.

This humorous parody pokes fun at the Hong Kong-style kung-fu movies from the '70s. Great fun, but very silly!

There are two Easter eggs to find on this DVD. From the main menu, scroll down and select "Special Features." Once inside, press the Up Arrow three times and a red icon of the "Matrix Cow" will appear. Press Enter to see a dramatic slow-motion sequence of the cow-nipple flick. Look, we didn't say this was a *cool* Easter egg!

The other one is a little better: Go back to the "Special Features" section. Enter the submenu entitled "Cut Scenes" near the bottom of the screen. Once inside, highlight the words "The Evil Council Loves Tacos" near the bottom of the screen, but don't press Enter just yet. Instead, press the Right Arrow once on the DVD remote and a red silhouette of a man will appear. Now press Enter to watch funny outtakes of a funky "Chosen One" with his dancing loins. Silly, yes.

L.A. Story

Artisan/TriStar Pictures ★ **Released** 1991 ★ **Directed by** Mick Jackson ★
Starring Steve Martin, Victoria Tennant, Richard E. Grant, Marilu Henner,
Sarah Jessica Parker

Zany TV weatherman Harris Telemacher (Steve Martin) is looking for love, happiness, and a meaning to his questionable existence. Can this be achieved in—of all places—Los Angeles? This romantic comedy was also written by Steve Martin.

The *L.A. Story* DVD houses a handful of gratifying Easter eggs. From the main menu, press the Left Arrow and the Cadillac's taillights will turn red. Press Enter to watch a hidden interview with director Mick Jackson about the Harris Telemacher character in the film.

Next, from the main menu, select "Special Features" from the middle of this screen. When the next screen appears, press the Left Arrow on the DVD remote and the bright words "Kiss Her" will appear in the sign. Now press Enter to watch a hidden interview with Steve Martin on how he came up with the idea behind *L.A. Story*.

There are three other Easter eggs on this disc.

Access the "Cast & Crew" section from the main menu. Click the name "Steve Martin" to read about his career. Once inside, press the Up Arrow on the remote and Martin's sunglasses will turn purple. Press Enter to see an interview snippet with co-star Victoria Tennant talking about Martin.

Now go back to "Cast & Crew" and select Victoria Tennant's bio. Press the Up Arrow once inside and some musical notes will appear at the top of the screen. Press Enter and it'll play a little ditty for you (on a tuba, no less) before playing more of the interview with Tennant.

Lastly, select "Mick Jackson" from the "Cast & Crew" screen (he's last on the list) and then press the Up Arrow once inside. A lightning bolt will appear in the upper right-hand corner of the screen. Press Enter; you'll hear thunder crash, and then Jackson will talk more about the "enchanting" and "magical" city that is Los Angeles.

Lara Croft in Tomb Raider

Paramount Pictures ★ Released 2001 ★ **Directed by** Simon West ★ **Starring** Angelina Jolie

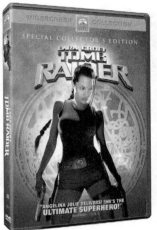

This video game-turned-movie casts the sexy Angelina Jolie as British adventurer Lara Croft, resolute to save the world by stopping a time-controlling talisman and ancient key from falling into the wrong hands.

And what sci-fi action flick would be complete without an Easter egg planted on its DVD?

From the main menu, go to the "Special Features" section, and press the Down Arrow on the remote two times. The two waves at the bottom of the screen will stop flashing (below the words "Main Menu").

Press Enter for an emotional two-minute interview clip with Jolie and her real-life dad, Jon Voigt, talking about working together on this film.

The Last Starfighter

Universal Pictures ★ Released 1984 ★ **Directed by** Nick Castle ★ **Starring** Lance Guest, Dan O'Herlihy, Catherine Mary Stewart, Robert Preston

This sci-fi flick from the mid-'80s tells of a teenage video-game wizard recruited to help fight a war in outer space to protect the universe. Talk about "Space Invaders"!

Well, there's a hidden trailer on this DVD—if you know where to find it. From the main menu, scroll down to "Bonus Materials" and then click on the little yellow arrow at the bottom of the screen to go to page 2. Now click on "Cast & Filmmakers." Once inside, go to the section for director Nick Castle, and on the fourth page of his biography/filmography, you'll notice that the film *Major*

Payne has a film reel beside it. Navigate over to it and press Enter to watch a trailer for this 1995 comedy, directed by Castle after he made *The Last Starfighter*.

The Lawnmower Man

New Line Cinema ★ Released 1992 ★ **Directed by** Brett Leonard ★ **Starring** Jeff Fahey, Pierce Brosnan, Jenny Wright

A brilliant scientist, Dr. Lawrence Angelo (Pierce Brosnan), uses an experimental virtual-reality treatment on the simple lawnmower man, Jobe Smith (Jeff Fahey). But unbeknownst to Dr. Angelo, his company alters the software and switches the enhancement drugs in the hopes of engineering a relentless killing machine.

The instant cult classic features a hidden puzzle game.

Insert the "Movie" side of the disc, and then select "Special Features" from the main menu. Scroll down to "The Cast" and instead of pressing Enter, press the Left Arrow. You'll see eight lime-green hexagons lit up to the left of the screen. Press Enter.

Courtesy of New Line Home Entertainment, 2003.

Enjoy this puzzle memory game comprised of yellow, blue, and red hexagons. Selecting the right piece in the correct order will flash "Access Granted" on the screen; selecting the wrong pieces will flash "Access Denied."

Complete the entire sequence and you'll see the words "You've Beaten the Lawnmower Man!" along with a humorous animated graphic.

Did You Know?

Wow! *Tomb Raider* is one of the most popular computer and console video game series of all time. Since its debut in 1996 (on the Sony PlayStation, Sega Saturn, and PC), the game series has sold more than 28 million units worldwide. The latest in the franchise, dubbed *Lara Croft: Tomb Raider—The Angel of Darkness*, debuted in June of 2003.

Liar Liar: Collector's Edition

Universal Studios ★ Released 1997 ★ **Directed by** Tom Shadyac ★ **Starring**
Jim Carrey, Jennifer Tilly, Swoosie Kurtz, Amanda Donohoe

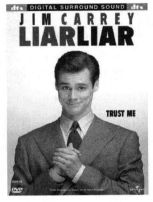

©1997 Universal City Studios, Inc.

A lawyer who isn't allowed to lie? This is grounds for a good comedy. Attorney Fletcher Reede (Jim Carrey) must tell the truth in and out of the courtroom for an entire day, thanks to his son's magical birthday wish.

The DVD "Collector's Edition" of *Liar Liar* contains a few hidden trailers to other Universal movies.

From the main menu, scroll up above the word "Play," and press Enter over "Bonus Materials." On the second page of these materials, select "Cast and Filmmakers" and scroll all the way to the bottom to select "Directed by Tom Shadyac." (An easier way is to press the Up Arrow once!) Press the Right Arrow three times, and you'll find two video trailers to other Shadyac films, including the 1996 remake of *The Nutty Professor* and *Patch Adams* (1998).

Life

Universal Pictures ★ Released 1999 ★ **Directed** by Ted Demme ★ **Starring**
Eddie Murphy, Martin Lawrence

©2003 Universal Studios Home Video.

Fast-talking con artist Rayford Gibson (Eddie Murphy) and an ambitious bank teller (Martin Lawrence) are sent to jail for life for a murder they didn't commit. Doesn't sound like a comedy, does it? Well it is. And this DVD features two funny Easter eggs, too.

From the main menu, select "Bonus Materials" and then head over to the second page by selecting "More." Now click on "Cast and Filmmakers" and choose "Eddie Murphy." Click "More" a few times to scroll through this filmography.

Undocumented trailers lie inside for *Bowfinger* (1999) and *The Nutty Professor* (1996).

The Limey

Artisan Entertainment ★ Released 1999 ★ **Directed by** Steven Soderbergh ★ **Starring** Terence Stamp, Lesley Ann Warren, Luis Guzman, Barry Newman, Peter Fonda

Relentless British ex-con Wilson (Terence Stamp) travels to Los Angeles to investigate his daughter's so-called "accidental" death. Wilson's prime suspect is the wealthy music promoter Terry Valentine (Peter Fonda), who had had an affair with Wilson's daughter.

Let's face it—chances are you haven't read many of those dry and boring crew or cast biographies found on most of today's DVDs, right? Well, the creators of the DVD for *The Limey* thought they'd spice up the section for you.

Courtesy of Artisan Home Entertainment Inc.

From the disc's main menu, select "Special Features" and then choose the "Cast & Crew" option. Once inside, choose the biography of producer Scott Kramer—but don't expect to read his real bio. Instead, a humorous, fictitious one is posted.

For example, one line says, "In 1978, when he was eighteen, Kramer's family traded him to a religious group of tool salesmen for a wrench and a can of hairspray." This faux bio is three pages long.

Little Nicky

New Line Cinema ★ Released 2000 ★ **Directed by** Steven Brill ★ **Starring** Adam Sandler

It's not easy being the son of the Devil. Little Nicky (Adam Sandler) must visit Earth for the first time to find and bring back his two rebellious brothers, who have escaped the underworld and are raising hell in New York City. Can this lovable misfit really save humanity?

There are a couple of well-hidden Easter eggs on this New Line Platinum Series disc.

From the main menu, select the "Special Features" sign. You'll now have three possible paths—choose the middle one ("Central Park"), and an image of Little Nicky on a park bench will appear. Rather than selecting from the list of features to the right, move down to the word "Documentaries," and then press the Left

Arrow. Now a yellow halo will appear over Little Nicky's head. Press Enter and enjoy an extensive trailer to New Line's fantasy film *The Lord of the Rings*.

Now go back to the "Special Features" menu, and do the same thing again—press the Left Arrow when the word "Documentaries" is highlighted so that a yellow halo appears over Sandler's head. Instead of pressing Enter, press the Left Arrow, then the Down Arrow, and then the Right Arrow, and a special interactive version of the movie will begin. Press the right Skip button, and some information will be available on the bottom of the screen.

You can now press Enter at various points in the film (or press the right Skip button often) to read biographies, see hidden interviews, watch deleted scenes and music videos, and much more.

Highlights include alternate Rodney Dangerfield lines, bloopers "from hell," veteran rock stars discussing the origins of heavy metal and why it was an important part of this film, a disturbing dart scene, and extra Jon Lovitz material.

Lastly, go back to the main menu of the DVD, and scroll down to highlight the words "Scene Selection." Now press the Right Arrow, and the Infinifilm logo will turn white. Press Enter to read the DVD credits for this disc.

Logan's Run

Warner Bros. ★ Released 1976 ★ **Directed by** Michael Anderson ★ **Starring** Michael York, Richard Jordan, Jenny Agutter, Roscoe Lee Browne, Farrah Fawcett, Michael Anderson Jr., Peter Ustinov

In this sci-fi adventure, citizens of a confined, futuristic world are not permitted to live past the age of 30. Logan 5 (Michael York) is a policing "Sandman" responsible for chasing down and apprehending "Runners"— those who try to escape. But with the help of his love interest, Jessica 6 (Jenny Agutter), Logan discovers the truth about this society and decides to escape and seek out a place known as "Sanctuary," where people are free.

Fans of this classic film will enjoy the egg planted on the disc.

From the DVD's main menu, press the Right Arrow on the DVD, and the crystal in the hand will turn purple. Now press Enter to read the *Logan's Run* Life Clock description and images. For example, a white crystal means the bearer is 8 years of age or younger. Yellow is for ages 9 through 15; green means ages 16 to 23; and red is for ages 24 to Lastday (that is, 30 years old).

Watch the movie again and take note!

The Lord of the Rings: The Fellowship of the Ring—Extended Edition

New Line Cinema ★ Released 2001 ★ **Directed** by Peter Jackson ★ **Starring** Elijah Wood, Ian McKellen, Viggo Mortensen, Sean Astin, Ian Holm, Liv Tyler, Christopher Lee

Courtesy of New Line Home Entertainment, 2003.

This award-winning film adaptation of J.R.R. Tolkien's literary masterpiece follows the adventures of a young Hobbit named Frodo who has been entrusted to protect an ancient ring. But the power it yields is too great, so to prevent it from falling into the wrong hands, Frodo and his friends embark on an epic journey in order to destroy it.

There are two good eggs on this four-disc edition of *The Lord of the Rings: The Fellowship of the Ring*.

Insert the first DVD and choose "Select a Scene" from the main menu. Scroll to the last page (25 – 27) and navigate down to the words "The Council of Elrond." Now press the Down Arrow on the DVD remote and a gold ring will appear on the screen. Press Enter to watch a humorous "alternative" version of this famous scene, cooked up by MTV. Hilarious!

Another egg can be found on the second DVD. Pop in the disc, and from the main menu once again click on "Select a Scene" and choose the last page (Chapter 48). Scroll over to the number 48 and press the Down Arrow on the DVD remote. Two towers will appear. Press Enter to watch a theatrical trailer for the film *The Lord of the Rings: The Two Towers*, introduced by director Peter Jackson.

Lost in Space

New Line Cinema ★ **Released** 1998 ★ **Directed by** Stephen Hopkins ★
Starring William Hurt, Gary Oldman, Mimi Rogers, Heather Graham

In this remake of the popular '60s TV series, the Robinson family sets off into space to begin colonizing the planet Alpha Prime, when a stowaway sabotages the mission, thus causing the ship to become "lost in space."

There are a couple of hidden goodies buried on this DVD.

The first is a secret trivia game—pop the disc into the player, and from the main menu, select "Features" and then "Your Mission." Players are then asked to take control of the Jupiter 2 ship and lead the Robinson family to Alpha Prime. To achieve this, enter the correct info into the ship's onboard computer to activate the hyperdrive. The information to enter—which includes trivia tidbits on the movie, the cast, and the original show—can be found elsewhere on the disc.

Completing the entire game correctly will unlock a very funny joke reel of outtakes from the film and other gags with the cast.

Now head back to the main menu, and use the Right Arrow on the remote until the small New Line Cinema logo (on the right of the screen) is illuminated. Press Enter to be taken to a credits screen, and press Enter again over 'JVC digital Cybercam" to watch a short commercial with Buzz Aldrin—the second man on the moon (just behind Neil Armstrong)—promoting the JVC Cybercam digital camcorder.

Lastly, from the main menu, select "Features" and then "Jupiter II Crew." You'll find a hidden trailer to the film *Dark City* on the fifth page of William Hurt's biography. Press Enter to play it. Same goes for Mimi Rogers' entry—on the third and final page of her bio, you'll find a trailer to *Austin Powers: International Man of Mystery*.

Did You Know?

Director Robert Altman's son, Mike Altman, wrote the lyrics to the classic theme song for M*A*S*H—at age 14!

M*A*S*H

20th Century Fox ★ Released 1970 ★ **Directed by** Robert Altman ★ **Starring** Donald Sutherland, Elliott Gould, Tom Skerritt

In this blockbuster movie that spawned the beloved '70s TV series of the same name, *M*A*S*H* observes the hilarious antics of three Korean War army surgeons at their Mobile Army Surgical Hospital (MASH).

Insert the first disc of this two-DVD set, and from the main menu, scroll down once and select "Special Features." Now scroll down four times until the THX logo is highlighted and press the Right Arrow. A small yellow helicopter will appear on the screen. Press Enter to watch an entertaining and extended Spanish trailer to the film.

Also, from the main menu on both discs, select some of the signs on the right side of the screen (such as "Officer's Mess" and "Operating Theater") to be treated to various audio clips from the film. The two DVDs contain a total of about ten clips.

Hawkeye's Famous M*A*S*H Extra-Dry Martini Recipe

The following is Hawkeye's Famous M*A*S*H Extra-Dry Martini Recipe that's "guaranteed to put some Seoul in your Korea." This recipe was concocted by Fox Home Video and used as a promotion for the launch of the season one box set:

Ingredients: 1 Bottle Gin,   1 Bottle Vermouth

Additional Items Needed: 1 Hypodermic Needle,   1 Martini Glass
1 Jar Of Olives (If In Korea, Please Contact "Trapper" John McIntyre)
1 Official Camouflage Army Canteen

1. Insert hypodermic needle into opening of bottle of vermouth.
2. Remove a minute amount of vermouth.
3. Empty contents of needle into martini glass.
4. Swirl vermouth in glass. Be sure to cover all surface area of glass.
5. Empty contents of glass.
6. Pour gin into glass.
7. Add olive.
8. Enjoy beverage.
9. Repeat steps 1–7 until content.
10. Pass out.

Mad Max: Special Edition

MGM ★ **Released** 1979 ★ **Directed by** George Miller ★ **Starring** Mel Gibson

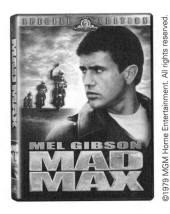

In Mel Gibson's second film—about a grim, lawless society in the near future—his character, Max Rockatowsky, seeks revenge for the murder of his family by a savage motorcycle gang.

There are a few cool surprises buried deep within the "Special Edition" of this DVD.

On the main menu, press the Up Arrow three times until the big red words "Mad Max" appear at the top of the screen. Press Enter to view five hidden sections about the cars from the film: the Black Interceptor, Yellow Pursuit, Yellow Interceptor (1), Yellow Interceptor (2), and The Night Rider.

Each entry features a thorough description (including year and model, and where in the movie it appeared) and three images from the movie (totaling 15).

Here's another egg on the same page: Highlight the word "Yellow Interceptor (1)," but do not press Enter just yet. Instead, tap the Left Arrow, and the headlights on the three cars in the picture will turn red. Now press Enter to read some info on Goose's '77 Kawasaki motorcycle in the film, with three action shots as well.

Made: Special Edition

Artisan Entertainment ★ **Released** 2001 ★ **Directed by** Jon Favreau ★ **Starring** Jon Favreau, Vince Vaughn, Sean "P. Diddy" Combs, Famke Janssen, Faizon Love, Vincent Pastore, Peter Falk

In this crime comedy, two lifelong friends and smalltime hustlers are hired by mob boss Max (Peter Falk) to go to New York for a "job," in order to prove themselves.

Pop in the DVD, and from the main menu, enter the section "Special Features," and then select "More *Made* Footage." Once inside, select "Alternate Scenes"; the last entry on this page is "Double Cross." Scroll down to highlight the words, and press the Left Arrow. A small *M* will appear on the screen.

Press Enter and nothing will happen—but don't worry—you need to spell the word "Made."

Now press the Left Arrow, and a pink *A* will appear. Press Enter. Now press the Right Arrow, and the *D* will appear; press Enter. Press the Left Arrow on the remote and an *E* will appear. Now press Enter again and nothing will happen until you press the Right Arrow one more time. The entire word "MADE" will now be spelled out—click Enter to view a much sexier version of the bachelor party lap-dance scene from the movie (Warning: Nudity).

If you're having trouble accessing this racy scene, there's another way to view it. Select the words "Double Cross" from the "Alternate Scene" section, and when this video begins, press the right Skip button on the remote once to launch the lap-dance sequence.

Magnolia

New Line Cinema ★ Released 1999 **★ Directed by** Paul Thomas Anderson ★ **Starring** Jeremy Blackman, Tom Cruise, Melinda Dillon, Philip Baker Hall, Philip Seymour Hoffman, Ricky Jay, William H. Macy, Alfred Molina, Julianne Moore, John C. Reilly, Jason Robards, Melora Walters

By coincidence or divine intervention, the lives of nine people cross paths in this extraordinary tale of courage, guilt, remorse, love, faith, and fate.

Insert the first of the two DVDs, and wait until the main menu appears. One of your choices will be "Set Up"—select this and then choose the "Color Bars" section. You'll see those familiar colored bars ("as seen on TV"), but wait for a few seconds until the bars disappear. Now kick back and enjoy close to ten minutes of bloopers from the film, including some comical Tom Cruise mess-ups.

Did You Know?

Allegedly, director Paul Thomas Anderson wrote most of the script while at actor William H. Macy's cabin in Vermont because he was too afraid to face a snake outside.

Mallrats: Collector's Edition

Universal Pictures ★ Released 1995 **★ Directed by** Kevin Smith **★ Starring**
Shannen Doherty, Jeremy London, Jason Lee, Claire Forlani

This cult classic takes place—where else—at the mall, where two friends, T.S.
Quint (Jeremy London) and Brodie Bruce (Jason Lee), decide to hang out
after being dumped by their respective girlfriends. To help win them back, their
dysfunctional buds, Jay (Jason Mewes) and Silent Bob (Kevin Smith), come up
with a surefire scheme.

©1995 Universal City Studios, Inc.

From the main menu, select "Bonus Materials"
and then choose "Deleted Scenes." Now press the
Right Arrow four times until the robot's eyes turn
red. Then press Enter.

Smith and a colleague will tease you and say,
"If you're here, you probably thought this was
going to be an Easter egg, something hidden. You
think you're so clever?"

Smith then says there is no such egg here, and to
go and buy some Jay and Bob merchandise instead!

Man on the Moon

Universal Studios ★ Released 1999 **★ Directed by** Milos Forman **★ Starring**
Jim Carrey, Danny DeVito, Courtney Love, Paul Giamatti

Jim Carrey, who won a Golden Globe award for this film, chronicles the personal
and professional life of the late eccentric comic, Andy Kaufman (best known
for his role in the '70s sitcom *Taxi*). Based on a true story, *Man on the Moon* delves
into the rise and fall of Kaufman's career, as well as his close relationships with
his manager, George Shapiro (Danny DeVito); his best friend and partner, Bob
Zmuda (Paul Giamatti); and his love interest, Lynne Margulies (Courtney Love).

Fans of Kaufman will certainly relish the hidden extras on this DVD.

From the main menu, scroll up to "Bonus Materials" and click Enter. Scroll
to the bottom of the page to the word "Andy," and press Enter to peruse through
a short biography on this unconventional comedian/actor/musician.

If you notice, many pages of this biography include a small black-and-
white picture of Kaufman, so press the Up Arrow, and an orange lining will

encircle the image. Press Enter to watch some entertaining video clips of Kaufman in action.

The section contains six clips.

Mars Attacks!

Warner Bros. ★ Released 1996 ★ **Directed by** Tim Burton ★ **Starring** Jack Nicholson, Glenn Close, Annette Bening, Pierce Brosnan, Danny DeVito

Tim Burton's sci-fi spoof on '50s UFO invasion movies features an all-star cast: Jack Nicholson, Glenn Close, Pierce Brosnan, Tom Jones, Danny DeVito, Annette Bening, Martin Short, Michael J. Fox, and Sarah Jessica Parker.

Why did these big-brained aliens come to Earth? For wanton destruction, of course. And what better place to start than Las Vegas.

There's a small but humorous Easter egg to be found on the DVD.

From the main menu, select the "Soundtracks" option, and you'll see the familiar choices: English, Spanish, French…and Martian!

Scroll down and press Enter over the "Martian" soundtrack option, and a new screen will appear with some graphics and funny Martian dialogue.

Did You Know?

Here's a small trivia tidbit: Did you know the sound effects used for the ray guns in *Mars Attacks!* were taken from Orson Welles' *The War of the Worlds*?

Did You Know?

Check out *Mallrats* for one of Kevin Smith's films that are all linked to one another in some way, shape, or form. In particular, *Clerks* (1994), *Mallrats* (1995), *Chasing Amy* (1997), *Dogma* (1999), and *Jay and Silent Bob Strike Back* (2001) are all part of Smith's "View Askewniverse" series, complete with interconnected characters, locations, and events. Visit www.viewaskew.com for more information.

The Master of Disguise

Columbia Pictures ★ Released 2002 **★ Directed by** Perry Andelin Blake **★**
Starring Dana Carvey, Brent Spiner, Jennifer Esposito, Harold Gould, James Brolin

In this adventure comedy for viewers of all ages, Pistachio Disguisey (Dana Carvey) is the "Master of Disguise" who can mysteriously transform into any number of memorable characters—be it George W. Bush, Turtle Man, or an old woman—in order to track down his parents' kidnappers.

The Easter egg is just as comical as the film. From the main menu, select "Special Features" and then choose "Featurettes." Once inside, press the Up Arrow twice to see a few funny outtakes from Turtle Man. Very funny, and there's a handful of them. And the lettuce and banana bit is just too much!

The Matrix

Warner Bros. ★ Released 1999 **★ Directed by** Andy Wachowski, Larry Wachowski **★ Starring** Keanu Reeves, Laurence Fishburne, Carrie-Anne Moss, Hugo Weaving

Easily one of the most influential sci-fi films in recent memory (especially in the special effects department), *The Matrix* stars Keanu Reeves as a savvy computer hacker who learns about the true nature of reality. He joins rebels Morpheus (Laurence Fishburne) and Trinity (Carrie-Anne Moss) as they attempt to overthrow the Matrix, a computer that runs the "world" as we know it.

From the main menu, scroll down and select "Special Features." Choose "The Dream World." See that little red pill on the bottom left of the screen? Good. Scroll down and click on it to watch a hidden six-minute documentary entitled "What is Bullet Time?"

While still in the "Special Features" area, click on the tab entitled "Cast & Crew." Select "Written and Directed by The Wachowski Brothers." You'll see another red pill, this time on the bottom right of the screen. Move to it and press Enter to view an 11-minute featurette, "What Is Concept?"

Lastly, also in the "Special Features" menu, select "Continue," and on the second page, select the "Follow the White Rabbit" mode. When you choose this, you can watch the entire movie again, but this time, whenever you see a white rabbit, select the icon to be taken to even more secrets embedded on the disc.

The Easter eggs hidden in *The Matrix* aren't too hard to find—after all, a white rabbit and a red pill are good clues taken right from the film—but they're rewarding nonetheless.

The Matrix Revisited

Warner Bros. ★ **Released** 2001 (based on *The Matrix,* 1999) ★ **Directed by** Josh Oreck ★ **Starring** Keanu Reeves, Laurence Fishburne, Carrie-Anne Moss, Hugo Weaving

Just like *The Matrix* DVD, this documentary disc also contains a few clever Easter eggs.

Enter the "Languages" section from the main menu, and then press the Left Arrow on the remote. A small phone booth will appear in the middle of the screen. Press Enter to play all 41 songs from this documentary. (You can listen to them in order as they're presented here or choose individual songs.)

Want to see the original (and extended) theatrical trailer to *The Matrix*? In this music jukebox area, stay on the screen highlighting songs 11 through 20. Press the Right Arrow on the remote, and a bullet will appear near Neo (Keanu Reeves). Now press Enter.

There are more eggs on this disc. To access them, enter the "Go Further" section from the main menu, and press the Right Arrow to watch clips of the "Woman in Red," Hugo Weaving's surgery, and Keanu Reeve's training.

Why not watch T2 and Motown on your PC?!

Two of Artisan Home Entertainment's DVDs from the first half of 2003—*T2—Extreme DVD* (page 157) and *Standing in the Shadows of Motown* (page 147)—each include a special Microsoft Windows Media 9 series enhanced DVD-ROM version of the film. The *T2* disc is presented in a high-resolution format for the ultimate in PC viewing, while the *Motown* DVD is in high-resolution, offering roughly three times greater resolution than standard DVD video. Cool stuff.

Me, Myself & Irene

20th Century Fox ★ **Released** 2000 ★ **Directed by** Bobby Farrelly, Peter Farrelly
★ **Starring** Jim Carrey, Renée Zellweger

In this hilarious comedy, Jim Carrey plays schizophrenic Rhode Island state trooper Charlie Baileygates, who falls in love with a wanted woman, Irene P. Waters (Renée Zellweger).

From the main menu, select "Bonus Features" and then choose "Deleted Scenes." Now press the Down Arrow until Carrey's face appears at the bottom of the screen. Press Enter and enjoy this collection of hilarious outtakes from the film.

Also, try this—go back to the main menu, and let the video clips play, but don't touch the remote for a minute or so. You'll then be asked if you need to take your medication. If you choose "Thanks, I Almost Forgot," it'll kick you back out to the main menu. However, if you click "No Thanks, I Feel Fine," the screen will shake and then "crazier" red menus, taunting music, and new video clips will appear!

Meet Joe Black

Universal Pictures ★ **Released** 1998 ★ **Directed by** Martin Brest ★ **Starring** Brad Pitt, Sir Anthony Hopkins, Claire Forlani, Jake Weber, Marcia Gay Harden, Jeffrey Tambor

A mysterious, uninvited stranger (Brad Pitt) pays a visit to the successful Bill Parrish (Sir Anthony Hopkins) a few days before his 65th birthday. "Joe Black" soon reveals himself as Death, but Parrish barters with him for some extra time on Earth.

Pssst—want to see a secretly hidden trailer? From the main menu, select "Bonus Materials." (Note: This means you need to take your eyes off Brad Pitt's face.) Once inside, scroll down twice and press Enter to access the "Cast and Filmmakers" section. On the fourth page of Brad Pitt's bio and filmography, there will be a film reel beside *12 Monkeys*, also starring Brad Pitt. Scroll over to it and press Enter to watch the theatrical trailer to the film.

Memento: Limited Edition

Columbia TriStar Home Video ★ Released 2000 ★ **Directed by** Christopher Nolan ★ **Starring** Guy Pearce, Carrie-Anne Moss, Joe Pantoliano

This exceptionally conceived and executed film tells of a man who suffers from short-term memory loss but is determined to track down his wife's killer.

And talk about a cool Easter egg—it allows viewers to watch the movie in chronological order. Here's how you do it: Pop in the second disc in this two-DVD set and watch the "psychological test" rotate through its pictures. Eventually it'll stop on a screen with 24 pictures. Don't touch anything and you'll hear random lines from the film. No, that's not the Easter egg!

Select the clock out of all these images and you'll be presented with multiple-choice questions. Select answer "C" for all questions, and another test will appear on the screen asking you to place the pictures of a woman changing her tire in chronological sequence. The answer is to put them in reverse order (3, 4, 1, and then 2). If you do this correctly, the movie credits will roll backwards and the film will then play in chronological order.

Mercury Rising

Imagine Entertainment/Universal Pictures ★ Released 1998 ★ **Directed** by Harold Becker ★ **Starring** Bruce Willis, Alec Baldwin, Chi McBride, Kim Dickens

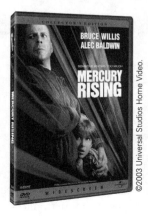

FBI agent Art Jeffries (Bruce Willis) fights against his own people to protect an autistic nine-year-old boy who has cracked the government's "unbreakable" encryption. Alec Baldwin plays ruthless Program Chief Nick Kudrow, who wants this threat eliminated.

Naturally, the Easter egg on this DVD relates to the film.

From the main menu, select "Bonus Materials" and then click on the little arrow to go to the second page of extras. Here, scroll down to "Theatrical

Trailer" and press the Left Arrow on the DVD remote—Simon's magazine will say "Crack the Code." Now press Enter to have fun deciphering the codes, and you'll be rewarded for doing so successfully.

The Mexican

DreamWorks Pictures ★ **Released** 2001 ★ **Directed by** Gore Verbinski ★ **Starring** Brad Pitt, Julia Roberts, James Gandolfini

This romantic comedy stars Brad Pitt as Jerry Welbach, who is torn between his girlfriend Samantha Barzel (Julia Roberts) and mob boss Winston Baldry (James Gandolfini). Welbach promises Barzel he'll end his criminal ways but must go to Mexico for Baldry to retrieve a priceless—and allegedly cursed—antique pistol known as "The Mexican."

TM & ©2001 DreamWorks L.L.C., reprinted with permission by DreamWorks L.L.C.

From the main menu of this DVD, scroll down twice and select the "Special Features" page. Then scroll down to the "Cast" section, and choose the biography for Brad Pitt.

Beside his name at the top of the screen, you'll notice a filmstrip. Press the Up Arrow on the DVD remote, and the filmstrip will turn from red to yellow. Press Enter to watch a lengthy deleted scene where Welbach (Pitt) is attempting to call Barzel (Roberts) from a Mexican pay phone, but gets her answering machine instead.

Miss Congeniality

Warner Bros. Pictures ★ **Released** 2000 ★ **Directed** by Donald Petrie ★ **Starring** Sandra Bullock, William Shatner, Ernie Hudson, Michael Caine, Benjamin Bratt, Candice Bergen

In this critically acclaimed comedy, FBI agent Gracie Hart (Sandra Bullock) goes undercover in order to stop a terrorist targeting a Miss United States beauty pageant.

There are some hidden deleted scenes buried on this disc—if you know where to look, that is. From the main menu, enter the "Special Features" section. Then click on "Documentaries." There are two documentaries to choose from here—

"Preparing for the Pageant" and "The Pageant: Behind the Crown." If you watch each one to the very end, you'll be treated to a deleted scene following each documentary. After the eight-minute "Preparing for the Pageant" documentary is a hilarious dancing scene narrated by director Donald Petrie. And following the ten-minute "The Pageant: Behind the Crown" is a deleted wedding scene and "The De-Throning of Miss New Jersey," narrated by the director, who also explains why the scene was eventually cut.

Monkeybone

20th Century Fox ★ Released 2001 ★ **Directed by** Henry Selick ★ **Starring** Brendan Fraser, Bridget Fonda, Chris Kattan

In this comedy, cartoonist Stu Miley (Brendan Fraser) falls into a coma, unleashing Monkeybone, his racy alter-ego who is determined to wreak havoc on the real world. Miley must catch Monkeybone before his sister pulls the plug on him, while avoiding Death (portrayed by Whoopi Goldberg!).

The film combines stop-motion animation with live action to deliver a unique visual experience.

OK, now on to the Easter egg....

From the main menu, select "Language Selection" and once inside, press the Right Arrow. A monkey holding a sign will appear advising, "Press Play to See the Organ Harvest."

Press Enter to be treated to a special behind-the-scenes video showing how the organ-donor scene in the movie was achieved.

Look for More Final Destination I and II Online

Even though New Line Home Entertainment's DVD for this teenage thriller—and its sequel, *Final Destination 2*—is chock-full of extra features for fans of the film, there's an opportunity to see even more on the Internet. The original theatrical web site—www.deathiscoming.com—has been updated by New Line to include clips of deleted scenes, documentaries, and the audio commentary. Now that's adding more bang for the buck.

Monster's Ball

Lions Gate Films ★ **Released** 2001 ★ **Directed by** Marc Forster ★ **Starring** Billy Bob Thornton, Heath Ledger, Halle Berry

Hank Grotowski (Billy Bob Thorton) is a bigoted prison guard who reexamines his beliefs after falling in love with Leticia Musgrove (Halle Berry), the wife of a recently executed black prisoner.

Berry took home the coveted "Best Actress in a Leading Role" Oscar at the 2002 Academy Awards for her performance in this film.

From the main menu, highlight the words "Play Movie," but don't press Enter just yet. Instead, press the Up Arrow, and a secret Lion's Gate Entertainment logo will appear on the screen. Press Enter to be treated to a trio of trailers to other Lion's Gate films: *Chelsea Walls, The Rules of Attraction,* and *The Cat's Meow.*

Now go back to the main menu and select "Special Features." Once inside, press the Up Arrow and a small logo will appear for American Cinematheque. Press Enter to watch a lengthy preview of *Everything Put Together* (2000), another film by director Marc Forster.

Monsters, Inc.

Walt Disney Pictures/Pixar Animation Studios ★ **Released** 2001 ★ **Directed by** Peter Docter, David Silverman, Lee Unkrich ★ **Starring** Billy Crystal, John Goodman, James Coburn, Jennifer Tilly, Mary Gibbs, Steve Buscemi, Sam "Penguin" Black

Monsters fuel their city by harvesting the screams of children—but ironically, these creatures are terrified to touch humans for fear of contamination. When an innocent child passes through to the monster world and befriends James "Sulley" Sullivan (John Goodman), both realize they have little to be afraid of.

There are a number of good Easter eggs planted on this award-winning computer-animated film. Insert the second DVD and select the "Monsters Only" door. Once inside, press the Right Arrow on the DVD remote and the eye inside the Monsters, Inc. logo will illuminate. Press Enter to be treated to a hilarious collection of animation test footage, outtakes, and gags, preceded by a real monkey placing Easter eggs into a basket and a personal message from director Peter Docter.

Now go back out to the main menu and this time select the "Humans Only" door. Click to watch the "Production Tour," and fast-forward all the way to the end. When it's finished, you'll see a number of doors placed on the screen. Have fun selecting all of these hidden Easter eggs—they include bloopers, sketches, animation tests, and funny scenes that never made it into the movie.

Lastly, go back out to the main menu and select "Humans Only" one last time. Once inside, highlight the "Pixar" door and then press the Down Arrow on the remote. Pressing Enter then will take you to a section of DVD credits.

Monty Python and the Holy Grail: Special Edition

Columbia Pictures ★ **Released** 1975 ★ **Directed by** Terry Gilliam, Terry Jones ★ **Starring** Graham Chapman, John Cleese, Eric Idle, Terry Gilliam, Terry Jones, Michael Palin

This classic film, starring Britain's most famous comedy troupe, chronicles the (mis)adventures of King Arthur and his devoted knights, who embark on a search for the Holy Grail.

This "Special Edition" DVD took a lot of time n' talent to put together—and the folks responsible for the work want to be recognized. So pop in the second (orange) DVD and from the main menu select "Sacred Relics" from the middle of the page. Once inside, navigate over to the words "Main Menu" but don't press Enter—instead, tap the Up Arrow on the DVD remote and the Holy Grail will be highlighted. Press Enter to read through the eight pages of DVD credits.

Moulin Rouge

20th Century Fox ★ **Released** 2001 ★ **Directed by** Baz Luhrmann ★ **Starring** Nicole Kidman, Ewan McGregor

One of the most memorable (and refreshingly distinctive) musicals of our time, *Moulin Rouge* takes place at the turn of the 20th century in Paris, where a lonely poet, Christian (Ewan McGregor), falls for the beautiful Satine (Nicole Kidman), the sexy star of the Moulin Rouge. A whopping 15 eggs are on *Moulin Rouge,* all on the second disc.

Ready? Here we go:

1. Click "More" to enter the second page. Press the Right Arrow five times, and a red fairy appears on the theater screen. Now press Enter to be taken to a silly dancing scene performed by the character Harold Zidler (played by Jim Broadbent).

2. From the main menu, select "The Cutting Room" and then click Enter. Tap the Right Arrow four times until a red windmill appears. Click Enter to view an outtake of McGregor serenading Kidman to Elton John's "Your Song."

3. Head to the submenu entitled "The Dance," and then select "The Dance" again. Highlight the section "A Word from Baz" and press the Right Arrow. A green fairy will appear beside this section. Press Enter to view a dance rehearsal.

4. Head to the submenu "The Design," and once inside, select "Costume Design" and then enter the section "A Courtesan's Wardrobe." Scroll to the fourth page, press the Up Arrow, and a green fairy will appear. Press Enter to watch another outtake with Kidman and McGregor.

5. Under the "The Music" submenu, scroll down and enter "The Lady Marmalade Phenomenon." Press the Right Arrow three times, and a red windmill will appear at the bottom of the screen. Press Enter for a scene with Baz Luhrmann driving in a car.

6. From the main menu, select "The Design" and once inside, press "1," and then "8" on the DVD remote (or if that doesn't work, "10+" and then "8"), and then "9" and "9" (1899 is the year the movie begins), and this'll launch some behind-the-scenes makeup footage of men getting their nipples brushed with rouge!

7. Stay in "The Design" and choose "Set Design" from the list. Now click on "Spectacular Spectacular," and scroll to the second page (with the words "Spectacular Spectacular" written on the picture). Once here, press the Up Arrow, and press Enter to watch Luhrmann introduce you to the magic of the soundstage.

8. While still in the "Set Design" area, choose "The Gothic Tower," and scroll over to the fifth page (using the Skip buttons). Press the Up Arrow and then press Enter for even more rehearsal footage with Kidman (in sexy glasses!) playing a joke on McGregor.

9. From the "Set Design" submenu, select "The Bohemians," and scroll over to the fifth page. Press the Up Arrow and press Enter to highlight the windmill. This will launch a cancan rehearsal.

10. From the main menu, select "Marketing" and then head to "Photo Gallery." Scroll down once to highlight the name "Mary Ellen Mark," and then press the Right Arrow; a red windmill will appear. Press Enter to view a

wardrobe fitting with John Leguizamo (who played Henri de Toulouse Lautrec in the film).

11. From the main menu, select "The Stars"; once this video clip ends, press 9 and then 1 and then 7 on the DVD remote (or "10+" and then "7") to access a hidden scene with three bagpipers— a surprise Luhrmann arranged for McGregor as a going-away present.

12. While still in "The Stars," press the Up Arrow when over Leguizamo's portrait, and a green fairy will appear. Press Enter to see Leguizamo dressed as an Indian sitar instrument.

13. From the main menu, select "This Story is About…" and select the third entry, "Old Storylines & Script Comparisons." Once inside, press the Right Arrow five times, and a green fairy will appear on the screen. Press Enter to see Luhrmann wielding a hammer as a joke.

14. From the main menu, select "The Dance" and then enter the section "Choreography." Once inside, press the Right Arrow three times, and a red windmill will appear to the right of the words "Main Menu." Press Enter to watch Luhrmann dance around a stage.

15. From the main menu, select "The Design" and then click on the last entry, "Smoke and Mirrors." Once inside, press 5 and then 1 and 8 on the DVD remote (or "10+" and "8" on some remotes), and this'll launch another rehearsal clip—this time of all the Parisian men throwing their top hats in the air at the club.

Did You Know?

This award-winning movie took 188 days to shoot, with 650 extras and over 750 crew members.

The enormous elephant (which was over 32 feet tall) used in the film took over two months to build…but only two days to destroy.

Cat Stevens' "Father & Son" was the only song that was refused permission to be included in the movie—allegedly, it was refused on religious grounds.

There were over 60 make-up and hair crew on the movie. And get this—over 85 colored wigs were designed and custom-made in Rome.

Nicole Kidman broke her rib twice while shooting the film. The first time was during preproduction, and the second was during filming while being fitted for a corset.

Mr. Deeds

Columbia Pictures/New Line Cinema ★ Released 2002 **★ Directed by**
Steven Brill **★ Starring** Adam Sandler, Winona Ryder, Peter Gallagher, Jared
Harris, Allen Covert, Erick Avari, John Turturro

Make your parents proud and bring home a billionaire! Based on the Academy
Award-winning Frank Capra classic, *Mr. Deeds* is a rags-to-riches tale of
a simpleminded pizza maker, Longfellow Deeds (Adam Sandler), who inherits a
whopping $40 billion from a long-lost relative. Nice, huh?

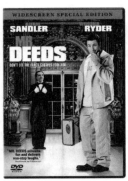

Here's how to access the Easter egg: From the
main menu, go to the "Special Features" option near
the bottom of the screen. Once inside, scroll down
to highlight the entry entitled "Music Video: Dave
Matthews Band, 'Where Are You Going?'" Now press
the Right Arrow twice on the DVD remote and the
icon that says "Mandrake Falls Fire Department
Volunteer" will become illuminated. Press Enter to
be treated to a cute clip with Adam Sandler at an
orchestra "jam session." Boy, he sure looks like he
enjoys his food!

The Mummy: Ultimate Edition

Universal Studios ★ Released 1999 **★ Directed by** Stephen Sommers **★
Starring** Brendan Fraser, Rachel Weisz

Three thousand years ago, the priest Imhotep
(Arnold Vosloo) was tortured and mummified
alive for sleeping with the Pharaoh's girlfriend.
Now, in 1923, he has returned to wreak havoc.
This ancient curse is accidentally unleashed as
adventurous French foreign legionnaire Richard
O'Connell (Brendan Fraser) and a band of treasure
hunters discover the lost city of Hamunaptra.

Music lovers will enjoy the Easter egg embedded
on this "Ultimate Edition" DVD of *The Mummy*.

From the disc's main menu, enter the section
entitled "Languages," and wait for a moment until the animation finishes. Now
turn up the volume, and put your feet on the coffee table—you can listen to
Jerry Goldsmith's movie soundtrack in its entirety.

Here's one more egg: Select the "Bio" section for actors Brendan Fraser and Arnold Vosloo to uncover secret trailers to the films *Darkman II* and *Gods and Monsters.*

The Mummy Returns

Universal Pictures ★ Released 2001 ★ **Directed by** Stephen Sommers ★
Starring Brendan Fraser, Rachel Weisz, John Hannah, Arnold Vosloo, Oded Fehr, Patricia Velazquez, Dwayne "The Rock" Johnson

This is the second film in this action/adventure series back by popular demand. This time around, an ancient legacy of terror is unleashed when the accursed mummy, Imhotep (Arnold Vosloo), is resurrected along with the Scorpion King (Dwayne Johnson). Back to save the world are Rick O'Connell (Brendan Fraser) and his wife, Evie (Rachel Weisz).

©2001 Universal Studios Inc.

From the DVD's main menu, scroll up to the "Bonus Materials" section, and once inside, enter the second page of features by pressing Enter over the word "More."

One of the entries will be "Egyptology 201"— select it and then choose the first entry, "An In-Depth Look at Mummification." Now press the Right Arrow on the DVD remote twice until a scorpion symbol turns red on the screen. Press Enter to watch a two-minute video about a 1994 mummification at the University of Maryland!

Another secret goodie is also on the second page of bonus materials. This time, press the Up Arrow twice, and the hieroglyphs above the word "Menu" will turn red. Press Enter to view the DVD credits.

Egg-stra Secrets on Some My Big Fat Greek Wedding DVDs

Know anyone "down under"? Now you can let them in on a secret. On the region 4 DVD of *My Big Fat Greek Wedding* (found in Australia, New Zealand, and Central and South America), there's a "squeaky clean" Easter egg to find. On the menu screen, click on "Previews" and then click the Left Arrow to highlight the Windex label on the bottle. Press Enter to watch an interview with Tom Hanks followed by recipes for Moussaka.

My Big Fat Greek Wedding

HBO ★ **Released** 2002 ★ **Directed by** Joel Zwick ★ **Starring** Nia Vardalos, John Corbett, Lainie Kazan, Michael Constantine, Gia Carides, Louis Mandylor, Andrea Martin, Joey Fatone

And you thought *your* family was crazy? This big fat comedy chronicles a 30-something, (gasp) unmarried Greek woman, Toula (Nia Vardalos), who falls in love with an "all-American," Ian Miller (John Corbett). Oddly, her eccentric family doesn't sway Miller's intentions of going through with the wedding plans.

The DVD for this off-Broadway-show-turned-box-office-success-story includes the feature film (presented in widescreen format), English and French audio, scene selection, and a handful of special features, including audio commentaries by director Joel Zwick and stars Vardalos and Corbett.

And of course, there's an Easter egg. Well, a small one, anyway. From the main menu, scroll down to the words "Special Features"—it's the last option on the screen. Now press the Right Arrow on the DVD and a secret "HBO" will appear in blue underneath the video montage. Press Enter to read the credits on the making of this DVD, including the folks responsible for authoring, menu design, and audio commentary.

The Ninth Gate

Artisan ★ **Released** 1999 ★ **Directed by** Roman Polanski ★ **Starring** Johnny Depp, Lena Olin, Frank Langella, James Russo, Jack Taylor, Emmanuelle Seigner

In this gothic thriller, Dean Corso (Johnny Depp) is a rare-book dealer who is hired to locate the last remaining copies of *The Nine Gates of the Shadow Kingdom*, a manuscript that can summon the Devil himself.

From the disc's main menu, head over to "Special Features," and once inside, highlight the word "Trailers" without pressing Enter. Instead, tap the Left Arrow and the words "TV Spot 1" will appear on the lower-left of the screen. Press Enter to view this *Ninth Gate* television commercial.

Now head back to "Special Features," and click the small arrow at the bottom to access the second page of bonus materials. Now scroll down to the bottom, and enter the section "Gallery Of Satanic Drawings." Once inside, click the little arrows at the bottom to get to the fourth gate, known as "Chance is not the same for all." On the second drawing/page of the fourth gate, the word "AT" will appear on the screen. Press the Up Arrow and the word will turn green. Press Enter to watch another TV spot for *The Ninth Gate*.

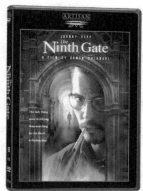

Head back to the second page of "Special Features," and select "Production Notes," second from the top. Once inside, scroll through to the tenth (and final) page, and then tap the Up Arrow. The words "TV Spot" will appear in the image. Press Enter to watch another promo for the film.

The last trailer for this movie is in the "Cast and Crew" section, on the second page of "Special Features." Head to the second page of cast and crew members (by selecting the little arrow at the bottom of the screen), and then choose "Michael Cheyko." On the third page of his bio, the word "AT" will appear on the screen again. Press the Up Arrow and the word will turn yellow. Now press Enter to watch a fourth trailer to the film.

Not Another Teen Movie

Columbia Pictures ★ Released 2001 **★ Directed by** Joel Gallen **★ Starring** Jaime Pressly, Mia Kirshner, Randy Quaid

This comedy spoofs popular teen flicks and overly used clichés with such characters as "the token black guy," "the beautiful weirdo," "the sensitive guy," "the foreign exchange student," and "the popular jock."

There are two Easter eggs hidden on the *Not Another Teen Movie* disc. From the main menu, scroll up once on the DVD remote and press Enter to select "Special Features." Now click on the little arrow to go to the second page of extras. Here, select the last entry, "Theatrical Trailers." If you can "stomach" this disturbing *American Beauty*-inspired image, scroll down and highlight the words "Special Features"—but don't press Enter. Instead, tap the Right Arrow on the DVD remote and a belly-button ring will appear. Press Enter to read the pre-clip explanation: "The footage that follows is not a deleted scene or an outtake or even a parody of any teen movie. Nathan West (the faux Freddie Prinze, Jr. on Janey's TV in the opening scene) is Chyler Leigh's real-life boyfriend. He and the crew have arranged a little surprise for her…." In this clip, West proposes to Leigh.

The second Easter egg can be found in the "Scene Selections" section. Go back out to the main menu and select this area—it's the middle entry. Once inside, press the Down Arrow once. The little yellow ducky will be illuminated and red lipstick marks will appear on Reggie Ray's (Ron Lestor's) behind. Press Enter to watch no less than four minutes of outtakes of the "Cruelest Girl in School" French-kissing the old woman. Eek! You've been forewarned.

Notting Hill

Universal Pictures ★ Released 1999 ★ **Directed by** Roger Michell ★ **Starring** Julia Roberts, Hugh Grant, Hugh Bonneville, Emma Chambers, James Dreyfus, Rhys Ifans, Tim McInnerny, Gina McKee

Anna Scott (Julia Roberts) is a successful movie star. William Thacker (Hugh Grant) is a stressed-out bookstore owner in the quaint town of Notting Hill. But both of their lives will be forever changed when their paths cross—and worlds collide.

Here's a neat little Easter egg that's a bit tricky to unlock. Using the DVD remote, start the movie and then access the secondary audio track to the film—there should be an option to switch audio tracks on your DVD remote (usually it's an "Audio" or "Options" button).

Now you'll hear the egg—it's French artist Charles Aznavour's version of the opening song, "She"—instead of the Elvis Costello version that plays on the regular version of the film. How cool! (Note: This will not work on "Notting Hill: Ultimate Edition.")

Nutty Professor II: The Klumps

Universal Pictures ★ **Released** 2000 ★ **Directed by** Peter Segal ★ **Starring**
Eddie Murphy, Janet Jackson, Larry Miller

We were introduced to the wacky Klump family in *The Nutty Professor,* and now they're starring in their own movie. Professor Sherman Klump (Eddie Murphy) falls for his colleague Denise Gaines (Janet Jackson) and discovers a formula that reverses aging. But once again, Sherman's thinner alter ego Buddy Love (Eddie Murphy, too) wants to take over, so the Klumps throw their weight around to bring Sherman back.

From the main menu, scroll over to "Bonus Materials" and enter the section. Then access the second page by clicking on the little red arrow. Now select "Recommendations" and on the second page you'll see a film reel underneath *The Nutty Professor.* Navigate over to it and press Enter to watch the hilarious theatrical trailer to this film.

O Brother, Where Art Thou?

Universal Pictures ★ **Released** 2000 ★ **Directed by** Joel Coen ★ **Starring**
George Clooney, John Turturro

In this tale, loosely based on Homer's *Odyssey,* three convicts escape a chain gang in the 1920s and set out in search of treasure. While on the run from the law, these mismatched criminals—the charming Ulysses (George Clooney), the hot-tempered Pete (John Turturro), and the slow-witted Delmar (Tim Blake Nelson)—inadvertently become a popular country music troupe along the way to finding their fortune.

The undocumented extra on this DVD is easy to find—simply pop in the disc, and don't touch anything at the main menu.

The instrumental music track that plays in its entirety in the background is a little-known tune from the *O Brother, Where Art Thou?* production featurette. Enjoy!

The Osbournes: The First Season

MTV Networks/Miramax Home Entertainment ★ Series Began 2002 ★
Starring Ozzy, Sharon, Kelly, and Jack Osbourne (as themselves)

This hit MTV reality series stars the quintessential heavy-metal god and his dysfunctional family. The DVD includes never-before-seen footage (previously edited out for TV), cast interviews, audio commentaries, a blooper reel, and a number of interactive Ozzy-themed games. Now that's something to bark at the moon about.

But there's also a hidden Easter egg. Pop in the second DVD and from the main menu head over to "Special Features" on the right-hand side of the screen. Here, select "Conversations with the Osbournes" and, once inside, highlight the last entry: "The Untold Story of Michael the Security Guard." Don't press Enter just yet—instead, tap the Right Arrow and the image of the baby will illuminate. Press Enter to be treated to a chat with Robert, the "newborn" Osbourne, and Kelly, too.

Osmosis Jones

Warner Bros. Pictures ★ Released 2001 ★ **Directed** by Peter Farrelly, Bobby Farrelly ★ **Starring** Chris Rock, Laurence Fishburne, David Hyde Pierce, Brandy Norwood, William Shatner, Molly Shannon, Chris Elliott, Bill Murray

This live-action/animated comedy stars a white blood cell cop, Osmosis Jones (voiced by Chris Rock) and his reluctant sidekick, Drix (voiced by David Hyde Pierce), who dive inside the body of Frank (Bill Murray) to combat a deadly virus named Thrax (Laurence Fishburne).

Catch all that? Good! Because we've got some eggs to find.

From the main menu, scroll down to "Smelly Feetures" (which will turn into "Special Features"). Press Enter to launch the new page. Once here, press the Left Arrow on the DVD remote. The freeway sign that says "Gas Next Exit" will illuminate in green. Press Enter for a cute clip from the movie.

Go back to the main menu and scroll down to the word "Lunguages" ("Languages"). Press Enter. Now go to the second page ("Continue") and press the Up Arrow—Drix's head will begin to glow. Press Enter to watch a lengthy montage of footage from the movie, set to music.

Wait—there's one more. Go back out to the main menu and access the section entitled "Frank's Gross Anatomy" (which will change to "Choose a Foul Scene" when it's highlighted). Press Enter to get to that section and then choose "The Earl of Hurl." Now press the Up Arrow once and a funny bone behind Bill Murray's head will turn green. Press Enter. Be forewarned, the last five seconds of this minute-long clip are pretty gross!

The Peacemaker

DreamWorks Pictures ★ Released 1997 **★ Directed by** Mimi Leder **★ Starring** George Clooney, Nicole Kidman

In this white-knuckle thriller, Colonel Thomas Devoe (George Clooney) and Dr. Julia Kelly (Nicole Kidman) put aside their personal differences to join forces and stop a terrorist from stealing nuclear weapons.

TM & ©1996 DreamWorks L.L.C., reprinted with permission by DreamWorks L.L.C.

From the disc's main menu, select "Special Features" and then choose the "Cast & Crew" option. Now select the bio of Clooney, which includes a secret interview snippet. To access it, press the Up Arrow, and Clooney's picture at the top of the screen will spawn a subtle green glow. Press Enter. Clooney talks about how he got the part for this film and why he accepted this role.

Now try the same thing for Kidman's bio and director Mimi Leder's bio (press the Up Arrow for each) to view even more behind-the-scenes interviews.

Pearl Harbor: The Director's Cut (Vista Series)

Touchstone Pictures ★ Released 2001 **★ Directed** by Michael Bay **★ Starring** Ben Affleck, Josh Hartnett, Kate Beckinsale, Alec Baldwin, Cuba Gooding Jr., Jon Voigt

In this epic World War II drama, childhood friends Rafe McCawley and Danny Walker (Ben Affleck and Josh Hartnett, respectively) decide to join the war and eventually find themselves in love with the same woman, Nurse Lt. Evelyn Johnson (Kate Beckinsale).

Here's how to access the Easter eggs on this collection: Insert the first DVD from this four-disc set, and from the main menu select "Set Up." Once inside, navigate over to highlight the words "Audio Options" but don't press Enter just yet. Instead, press the Down Arrow on the DVD remote and a red star will appear below the words. Press Enter to see—and read about—why you should watch this film in widescreen format.

This egg explains the following: "*Pearl Harbor* was photographed in anamorphic, which has an aspect ratio of 2.35:1, meaning the film image is 2.35 times wider than it is tall. Most televisions, by contrast, are square." Stefan Sonnenfeld, a colorist from Company 3, then explains and shows the significance of watching it at home the way it was shown in theaters.

The other egg can be found on the second disc. From the main menu, select "Special Features" near the bottom of the screen. Once inside, press the Right Arrow on the DVD remote and a red star will appear on the right-hand side of the screen (beside the Faith Hill music video option). Now press Enter to watch a funny 10-minute gag reel from the film, set to music. And this montage of bloopers has a cute introduction, too. Caution: foul language!

The Pink Panther

MGM ★ Released 1963 ★ **Directed by** Blake Edwards ★ **Starring** David Niven, Peter Sellers, Robert Wagner, Capucine

P eter Sellers plays clumsy Inspector Jacques Clouseau, who stumbles upon a jewel thief out to snatch Princess Dala's "panther."

Can this bumbling fool really solve the case? Can you find the Easter egg? Here's how: Pop in the disc (either side) and enjoy the classic Pink Panther music! When you're done, scroll down four times until the big words "The Pink Panther" turn from pink to baby blue. Press Enter to enjoy a copy of the original film poster from 1963. At the top of the poster it says, "You only live once so see the *Pink Panther* twice!"

C'est vrai!

The Pink Panther Strikes Again

MGM/United Artists ★ **Released** 1976 ★ **Directed by** Blake Edwards ★
Starring Peter Sellers, Herbert Lom, Colin Blakely, Leonard Rossiter,
Lesley-Anne Down

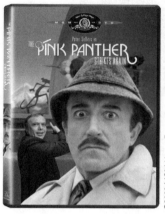

That bumbling French inspector is at it
again. Peter Sellers reprises his comical
role as Inspector Clouseau, and of course his
dumb luck may just stop a madman with a
doomsday device.

Fans of this film should enjoy its Easter
egg. From the main menu, scroll down using
the Down Arrow on the DVD remote four
times until *The Pink Panther Strikes Again*
logo at the top of the screen becomes
illuminated. Now press Enter to see two
original theatrical posters for the film.

Planet of the Apes

20th Century Fox ★ **Released** 2001 ★ **Directed by** Tim Burton ★ **Starring**
Mark Wahlberg, Tim Roth, Helena Bonham Carter

In this remake of the popular '60s sci-fi film and '70s TV series, *Planet of the
Apes* takes place in 2029, when an American astronaut Capt. Leo Davidson
(Mark Wahlberg) crash lands on a strange planet inhabited by talking apes.

Pop in the first disc of this two-DVD set, and from the main menu, select
"Special Features" and then choose "Commentaries." Now press the Down Arrow
twice, and a red monkey will illuminate in the middle of the screen. Press Enter
to watch a special commentary of the movie—in ape language!

Cute, but not as interesting as the second egg on this DVD.

In the last scene in the movie, where Davidson (Wahlberg) crash lands back
on Earth and is standing in front of the General Thade memorial, click Enter
when he's staring at the statue. A featurette will immediately launch, discussing
the making of the sculpture.

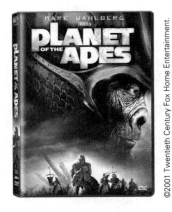

Also, go back to the "Special Features" section from the main menu, and enter the "Cast & Crew Profiles" area. Once inside, select "Cast" and then enter the bio for Estella Warren (who plays Daena in the film). Now press the Up Arrow, and the arrow below her picture will turn orange. Press Enter to be treated to Warren's first audition for the part.

First audition tapes for both Erick Avari ("Tival") and Luke Eberl ("Birn") can be accessed in the same way.

Lastly, go back to the main menu and select "Language Selection" at the bottom of the screen. Scroll down to highlight the words "Resume Film," and instead of pressing Enter, tap the Right Arrow. A monkey's head in red will appear in the corner; press Enter to read the DVD credits.

Practical Magic

Warner Bros. ★ Released 1998 **★ Directed by** Griffin Dunne **★ Starring** Sandra Bullock, Nicole Kidman

It's not easy being a witch. Just ask sisters Sally and Gillian Owens (Sandra Bullock and Nicole Kidman, respectively), cursed to have all the men they fall in love with sent to an early grave. With some "practical magic" taught by their aunts, perhaps they can put an end to this centuries-old curse.

Insert the second side of the disc ("Special Features"), and from the main menu, go to the "Special Features" section. Scroll to the middle of the screen, where the word "Cauldron" appears. Press Enter and a screen with some herbs will appear, such as rosemary, mint, lavender, and others.

The goal is to brew a secret potion like Sally and Gillian did in the film, by selecting the right ingredients in the correct order. (Hint: Not all ingredients are needed, and clues to the right herbs are given in the other areas of this DVD.)

Successfully adding the ingredients will open two enjoyable documentaries. One is a six-minute film entitled *Making Magic,* and the other is *Casting the Spell,* a nine-minute short film on the cast, story, and the making of the film.

The Princess Bride: Special Edition

MGM ★ Released 1987 ★ **Directed by** Rob Reiner ★ **Starring** Robin Wright, Cary Elwes, Mandy Patinkin, Billy Crystal

Fantasy meets comedy in Rob Reiner's classic tale about the beautiful Buttercup (Robin Wright), who is held captive and will be forced to marry a detestable prince. Little does she know that her childhood sweetheart Westley (Cary Elwes) is determined to rescue her (though he's supposed to be dead), with the aid of two zany companions.

From the disc's main menu, press the Up Arrow on the remote, and a turquoise gem will glow at the top of the screen. Press Enter to be taken to another screen with nothing but the heads of eight cast members.

Now use the Up, Down, Left, and Right Arrows to navigate among the heads; pressing Enter will cause the selected head to grow even bigger, and a sound bite from that character will play.

Also on this screen are two other gems on each side of the words "Main Menu" at the bottom. Use the remote keys to highlight them and they'll turn purple. Press Enter to hear more lines from the film.

The Producers: Special Edition

MGM ★ Released 1968 ★ **Directed by** Mel Brooks ★ **Starring** Mel Brooks, Gene Wilder, Dick Shawn, Zero Mostel

In this '60s film (now a Broadway hit), Max Bialystock (Zero Mostel) is a scheming producer who, with the help of his accountant, Leo Bloom (Gene Wilder), discovers that he could make money from investors by creating a theatrical flop. Ironically, "Springtime for Hitler" becomes a runaway success.

This disc includes seven Easter eggs in all. Gotta love that Mel Brooks character! From the main menu, highlight the words "Play Movie" but don't press Enter. Instead, press the Left Arrow on the DVD remote and the number "18" will light up. Press Enter to hear a hilarious collection of audio outtakes.

There are five more Easter eggs like this to find from the main menu, including behind-the-scenes and in-movie montages with silly audio clips. Here's how to find them: Use the DVD remote on the main menu screen to highlight other numbers and letters, such as "17," "9," "C," "$8.50," and "1968." Press Enter when these turn green.

There's one more Easter egg. From the main menu, highlight the words "Play Movie" but don't press Enter. Instead, press the Up Arrow on the DVD remote and the words "Springtime for Hitler" will illuminate in green. Press Enter to watch a never-before-seen psychedelic animation of Lee "Ulla" Meredith doing her sexy dance.

Raising Arizona

20th Century Fox ★ Released 1987 ★ **Directed by** Joel Cohen, Ethan Coen ★ **Starring** Nicolas Cage, Holly Hunter, John Goodman

In this unique comedy, an ex-con (Nicolas Cage) and an ex-cop (Holly Hunter) discover they're unable to conceive a child, so they decide to kidnap a quintuplet and hit the road. "Biology and other people's opinions conspired to keep us childless," believes H.I. (Cage).

While the Easter eggs are not exactly hidden, the back of the *Raising Arizona* box doesn't say it has any extra goodies— but there are two complete movie trailers for other celebrated Coen brothers films: *Miller's Crossing* (1990) and *Barton Fink* (1991). Access them by selecting "Special Features" from the main menu and scrolling to the bottom of the screen.

Red Dragon

Universal Pictures ★ **Released** 2002 ★ **Directed** by Brett Ratner ★ **Starring**
Sir Anthony Hopkins, Edward Norton, Ralph Fiennes, Harvey Keitel, Emily Watson,
Mary Louise Parker, Philip Seymour Hoffman

Based on the acclaimed Thomas Harris novel, *Red Dragon* may be the creepiest prequel in film history to date, serving as a disturbing introduction to the infamous Dr. Hannibal Lecter (Sir Anthony Hopkins) and the events leading up to the 1991 Best Picture Oscar winner *Silence of the Lambs.*

After capturing Dr. Lecter, FBI agent Will Graham (Edward Norton) retires but is called back to duty to hunt down another mysterious killer, "The Tooth Fairy" (Ralph Fiennes).

And talk about a creepy Easter egg! Pop in the second disc ("Bonus Disc") and from the main menu tap the Left Arrow on the DVD remote. The cursor will disappear and you'll be treated to a hypnotic audio message from Hannibal Lecter himself! It begins, "Shhhhh, don't move. You're in shock now. I don't want you to feel any pain...."

Yikes!

Repo Man

Anchor Bay Entertainment ★ **Released** 1984 ★ **Directed by** Alex Cox ★
Starring Harry Dean Stanton, Emilio Estevez

In this strange but amusing comedy, a young and troubled man named Otto (Emilio Estevez) is mentored by the "Repo Man." But he soon discovers there's a lot more to this underworld than meets the eye.

There are two Easter eggs on this disc. From the main menu, select "Extras" from the list of options. Once inside the submenu, don't press anything. Instead, put your feet up on the coffee table and enjoy the Spanish version of the classic "Secret Agent Man." This version is entitled "Hombre Secreto" by the Plugz.

Courtesy of Anchor Bay Entertainment ©2003. ©1984 Universal City Studios, Inc.

Next, while still in this "Extras" section, scroll to the right until the words "Talent Bios" are highlighted in green. Now press the Up Arrow and one of the dials on the car radio will turn green. Press Enter to watch a short video clip called "The Repo Man Code," with its rules to adhere to. Cute extra!

Requiem for a Dream

Artisan Entertainment ★ Released 2000 ★ **Directed by** Darren Aronofsky ★ **Starring** Ellen Burstyn, Jared Leto, Jennifer Connelly, Marlon Wayans, Christopher McDonald

Courtesy of Artisan Home Entertainment Inc.

This disturbing tale examines the lives of four Coney Island residents grappling with varying forms of addiction, denial, and depression. Ellen Burstyn's outstanding performance as a TV-obsessed widow won her a nomination for Best Actress in a Leading Role at the 2001 Academy Awards.

As with most other Artisan DVDs, the *Requiem for a Dream* disc features a few clever Easter eggs.

From the main menu, press the Up Arrow or Down Arrow on the remote until the words "Hear Tappy's Amazing Life Story!" are illuminated in yellow. Press Enter to view the complete five-minute infomercial from the movie.

Also, inside the chapter index, use the Right Arrow to move over to the "Chapters 21 to 24" section. Press the Up Arrow twice to watch a never-before-released part of Tappy's show on how to change your life. Here, fans of the film can find out what rule 3 was…though you may not like the sound of it.

Reservoir Dogs

Artisan ★ Released 1992 ★ **Directed by** Quentin Tarantino ★ **Starring** Harvey Keitel, Tim Roth, Michael Madsen, Steve Buscemi, Lawrence Tierney, Christopher Penn, Quentin Tarantino

In *Reservoir Dogs,* his first feature film, Quentin Tarantino turned Hollywood upside down with his unique direction (placing events out of chronological order and merging separate stories into one), not to mention his irreverent screenplay and memorable characters! Who could forget Mr. White, Mr. Pink, and Mr. Brown?

Courtesy of Artisan Home Entertainment Inc.

There's a clever—and rewarding—Easter egg on the original DVD release of *Reservoir Dogs.*

Pop in the disc, and from the main menu, head to the "Special Features" section. A picture of the cop tied to a chair in the warehouse will be on the screen. Instead of scrolling through the options, click the Right Arrow on the DVD remote, and an ear will appear. Press Enter to watch a 20-minute interview with director and writer Tarantino.

Reservoir Dogs: Special Edition

Artisan ★ Released 1992 ★ **Directed by** Quentin Tarantino ★ **Starring** Harvey Keitel, Tim Roth, Chris Penn, Steve Buscemi, Lawrence Tierney, Michael Madsen

Courtesy of Artisan Entertainment, Inc. All Rights Reserved ©2003.

This violent cult classic—with memorable characters portrayed by Harvey Keitel, Steve Buscemi, and Tim Roth—follows the misadventures of five complete strangers collaborating to pull off a diamond heist.

There are two Easter eggs to find on the second disc of this 10th anniversary-edition DVD. Insert the "Full Screen" disc and, from the main menu, choose "Special Features" and enter the section. Now choose the first option, "The Critics' Commentary." Once inside, press the Up Arrow on the DVD remote and the string of lights will illuminate. The egg is more than three minutes of rolling credits on the making of this DVD, complete with funkadelic music.

And now the *really* cool egg: While still on the second disc, select "Special Features" from the main menu and then select "K-Billy Radio." Once inside, choose the last channel on the right (by the number 16) and then press Enter. This will take you to "Reservoir Dolls," a reenactment of the classic ear-cutting scene—but played out with action figures! The real scene runs the entire time in a small corner on the screen. Funny and disturbing at the same time! And gotta love the song, "Stuck in the Middle with You."

Revenge of the Pink Panther

MGM/United Artists ★ Released 1978 ★ **Directed by** Blake Edwards ★
Starring Peter Sellers, Herbert Lom, Robert Webber, Dyan Cannon

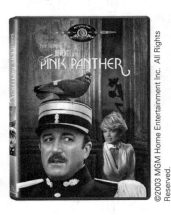

Believed to be dead, the clumsy Inspector Clouseau (Peter Sellers) heads to Hong Kong with a drug lord's mistress (Dyan Cannon) to probe a suspected heroin deal.

There's a fun Easter egg hidden on the disc, but you don't need to be a P.I. to find it: From the main menu, press the Down Arrow on the DVD remote and the words "Revenge of the Pink Panther" will light up. Press Enter to watch Inspector Clouseau morph into his various disguises from the film—complete with the classic *Pink Panther* instrumental music.

The Ring Has Two Sequels? Say What?

DreamWorks' creepy horror movie *The Ring* (page 123) is based on a little-known Japanese flick, *Ringu*. As in the U.S. version, people in the film die seven days after watching a disturbing videotape. The Japanese original debuted in 1998 and was based on a novel written by Kôji Suzuki published ten years earlier. Two Japanese movie sequels followed: *Ringu 2* (1999) and a prequel, *Ringu 0: Baasudei* (2000).

The Ring

DreamWorks SKG ★ **Released** 2002 ★ **Directed** by Gore Verbinski ★ **Starring** Naomi Watts, Martin Henderson, Brian Cox, David Dorfman, Lindsay Frost, Amber Tamblyn

Courtesy of DreamWorks Home Entertainment.

Arguably the scariest horror movie to surface in a long while, *The Ring* is about a deadly video tape that kills whoever watches it in seven days. OK, so the premise sounds silly, but good luck getting in a good night's rest after watching this flick.

The Ring features a scary Easter egg, too. Pop in the disc and from the main menu, press the Up Arrow and the cursor will disappear. Now press Enter to be treated to the disturbing (and deadly) video tape from the film. Even scarier is that a phone will ring a few seconds after you're taken back to the main menu—just as in the movie.

Don't worry—we won't tell if you jump!

Road Trip—Unrated

DreamWorks Pictures ★ **Released** 2000 ★ **Directed by** Todd Phillips ★ **Starring** Breckin Meyer, Seann William Scott, Amy Smart, Rachel Blanchard, Fred Ward, Tom Green

Courtesy of DreamWorks Home Entertainment.

In this adult comedy, four college friends set off on a cross-country road trip to retrieve a sexy videotape accidentally mailed to one of their girlfriends. Eek.

If you want to unlock the "fishy" Easter egg on this disc, you'll need a computer with a DVD-ROM drive in order to do so. Got it? Good. Let's proceed.... Pop in the disc and it'll ask whether you want to install the "PC Friendly" software. Choose "Yes" and follow the instructions. After a minute or so, a *Road Trip* menu will pop up with three options: "Play Movie," "Online Website," or "DVD-ROM Features." Don't select any of these—instead, use the mouse to click on the water tower in the upper right-hand corner of the screen. A singing fish will appear at the bottom, singing Tom Green's "The Salmon Song"!

Rocky

MGM ★ **Released** 1976 ★ **Directed by** John G. Avildsen ★ **Starring** Sylvester Stallone

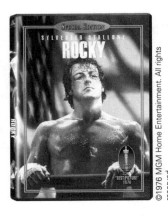

Rocky "The Italian Stallion" Balboa (Sylvester Stallone) is a small-time boxer who gets the chance to step into the ring with the heavyweight champ, Apollo Creed (Carl Weathers). With the help of his manager, Mickey Goldmill (Burgess Meredith), and his love interest, Adrian (Talia Shire), Rocky is determined to prove he can go the distance.

On the 25th anniversary edition DVD (also found in the *Rocky* box set), there's a humorous short film hidden within.

Simply pop in the disc and from the main menu, tap the Up Arrow on the remote. The word "Rocky" will illuminate toward the top of the screen. Now press Enter to watch an amusing clip entitled "Rocky Meets Stallone," where the actor Sylvester Stallone has a conversation with Rocky Balboa about what to do following the success of these boxing movies.

The Rocky Horror Picture Show

20th Century Fox ★ **Released** 1975 ★ **Directed by** Jim Sharman ★ **Starring** Tim Curry, Susan Sarandon, Barry Bostwick, Richard O'Brien

Let's do the "Time Warp" again—this time, on DVD.

This cult classic is based on the hit UK musical where a naive engaged couple—Brad (Barry Bostwick) and Janet (Susan Sarandon)—get lost on a rainy night and end up at a bizarre mansion crawling with extraterrestrial transsexual Transylvanians!

There are two cuts of the movie (U.S. and UK), but there's a hidden third version, too.

Pop in the first disc, and select either version of the film. From the main menu, scroll down to highlight the words "Scene Selection" (at the bottom of the screen), but don't press Enter. Instead, tap the Left Arrow, and a pair of yellow lips will appear in the bottom-left corner of the screen.

Now press Enter for a special treat—Richard O'Brien's original script indicated that the beginning of the film was to be shot in black and white as an affectionate nod to *The Wizard of Oz*. The film would only turn to color once Brad and Janet entered the world of the Transylvanians. Alas, this was decided against for a number of reasons, but this DVD does feature this rare, third version of the film.

Press Enter to play the movie.

Alternatively, there's an option to read the DVD credits from this screen.

Also, as an interesting note, press the Display button on the DVD remote during any of these three versions to find out which one you're watching. If you're in the first or second version, switching to 3 in the Display window is a shortcut that will immediately launch the Easter egg version.

Romeo + Juliet: Special Edition

20th Century Fox ★ Released 1996 **★ Directed by** Baz Luhrmann **★ Starring** Leonardo DiCaprio, Claire Danes

William Shakespeare's literary masterpiece is reborn in this brilliant remake, directed by visionary Baz Luhrmann (*Moulin Rouge, Strictly Ballroom*). This film chronicles the tragic love affair between Romeo (Leonardo DiCaprio) and Juliet (Claire Danes) and now takes place in Verona Beach during contemporary times.

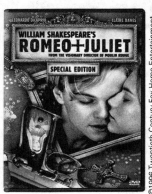

The "Special Edition" DVD contains audio commentary by Luhrmann, various making-of featurettes, and other behind-the-scenes material.

From the disc's main menu, simply press the Up Arrow on the DVD remote, and the little heart at the top of the screen will illuminate yellow. Press Enter to read a few pages of the DVD credits, followed by a shortcut to the "Director's Gallery" and the six clips within.

Ronin

MGM/United Artists ★ **Released** 1998 ★ **Directed by** John Frankenheimer ★ **Starring** Robert DeNiro, Jean Reno, Natascha McElhone, Stellan Skarsgård, Sean Bean, Jonathan Pryce

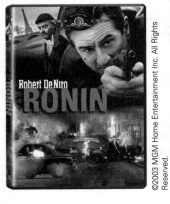

A group of covert intelligence agents become free agents and are commissioned to steal a top-secret briefcase—but this task proves to be a difficult one.

The Easter egg on the *Ronin* DVD can be a bit tricky to unlock but is worth it for fans of extra materials. From the main menu, start watching the feature film. Once the movie commences, use the DVD remote to access the title menus. Normally there will be a DVD button that says "Title," or "GoTo," or something of the sort.

Now select Title 22 (Note: You might need to press the 10+ button twice, then the number 2, and then Enter). Now you'll be able to watch a behind-the-scenes clip of a crew rigging up a car with cameras for stunt shots. Then when you return to the main menu you'll see that the footage shot with the car-mounted camera is the same used for the main menu screen.

The Royal Tenenbaums: The Criterion Collection

Touchstone Pictures/The Criterion Collection ★ **Released** 2001 ★ **Directed by** Wes Anderson ★ **Starring** Danny Glover, Gene Hackman, Anjelica Huston, Bill Murray, Gwyneth Paltrow, Ben Stiller, Luke Wilson, Owen Wilson

In one of the more distinctive and celebrated comedies of 2001, Royal Tenenbaum (Gene Hackman) makes an attempt to reunite with his estranged wife (Anjelica Houston) and dysfunctional yet brilliant children. Is it too little, too late? See for yourself in this feature-packed "Criterion Collection" edition DVD.

Oh yes, and there are two Easter eggs, too.

Insert the second DVD, and from the main menu, press the Up Arrow on the remote. A small on-screen arrow will point toward the words "The Criterion Collection" at the top of this page. Press Enter and Chas Tenenbaum (Ben Stiller) will take a break from shaving with his kids to welcome you to this special edition DVD.

Also on this second disc, select "Scrapbook" from the main menu and once inside, press the Down Arrow on the remote until the cursor points toward the Dalmatian mouse in the bottom left-hand corner of the screen. Press Enter to watch a silly deleted scene with Bill Murray goofing around.

Rush Hour

New Line Cinema ★ Released 1998 ★ **Directed by** Brett Ratner ★ **Starring** Jackie Chan, Chris Tucker

The fastest kick in the East meets the biggest mouth in the West in this blockbuster comedy about two mismatched cops determined to rescue the daughter of a Chinese diplomat.

And guess what—there's a fantastic Easter egg to uncover on this DVD. Problem is, it's very well hidden, and probably easier to find using a DVD-ROM drive rather than a standard DVD player.

Here's how to do it:

Once inside your PC's DVD software, start the movie, head over to Chapter 3, and then access Title 4. As you'll see, there's an early (and amateur!) Brett Ratner film, *Evil Luke Lee.*

When you find it, the director will congratulate you for your efforts before pleading "please, please, please don't show this to anyone!" Ratner then explains what you're about to see before the lengthy, humorous film begins to play.

Also, from the main menu, scroll to the bottom of the screen, and the Infinifilm logo will be highlighted underneath the option for "Scene Selections." Press Enter and the logo will turn yellow before jumping to a DVD production credits screen.

Did You Know?

Allegedly, Stallone wrote the script for *Rocky* (page 124) in just three days! Sylvester Stallone was a poor, out of work actor when he wrote this screenplay. Still, he refused to sell his script unless he was cast as the lead character.

Rush Hour 2

New Line Cinema ★ Released 2001 **★ Directed by** Brett Ratner **★ Starring** Jackie Chan, Chris Tucker

In this successful sequel, LAPD Detective James Carter (Chris Tucker) travels to Hong Kong for a well-deserved vacation, but once again finds himself solving crime alongside the acrobatic Chief Inspector Lee (Jackie Chan).

Pop in the DVD, and from the main menu, choose "Select A Scene." Look at the chapter numbers at the bottom of the screen. All but two of these pages feature three different scenes to jump to.

The first page with only two scenes has Scenes 7 and 8. Select this by pressing Enter over the numbers 7–8, and one of the three video-clip entries will be blank except for a red dragon. Use the remote to navigate over to this dragon, and press Enter to enjoy a lengthy widescreen trailer to *Lord of the Rings: The Fellowship of the Ring*, complete in 5.1 digital sound!

Now go to Scenes 15 and 16, and instead of a red dragon, there's a large number 7. Navigate over to it and press Enter to watch yet another anamorphic trailer for Peter Jackson's first *Lord of the Rings* feature film.

Lastly, go back to the main menu, press the Left Arrow on the DVD remote, and a small white Infinifilm logo will appear underneath the Chinese food take-out box. Press Enter to read the DVD production credits.

Did You Know?

Much of the movie takes place in the "Red Dragon" hotel, which was really the renovated Desert Inn in Las Vegas. The aging hotel was demolished in late 2001 after the movie was filmed. Director Brett Ratner's next film also happens to be named "Red Dragon," continuing the (mis)adventures of Dr. Hannibal "The Cannibal" Lecter (played by Sir Anthony Hopkins).

S1m0ne

New Line Cinema ★ Released 2002 **★ Directed by** Andrew Niccol **★ Starring** Al Pacino, Catherine Keener, Pruitt Taylor Vince, Jay Mohr, Rachel Roberts

Hollywood producer Viktor Taransky (Al Pacino) must find a replacement for an actress who has just walked off the set—so he creates one. *S1m0ne* follows the rise of a virtual star who becomes too popular to be kept a secret. Or can she?

There's a small Easter egg on this disc. Here's how to unlock it: From the main menu, press the Down Arrow on the DVD remote four times until the small white New Line logo in the corner of the screen is illuminated. Press Enter to read a credits and special thanks screen. Did ya know the documentary on this disc was produced by Organa? DVD production services were performed by Hollywood's LaserPacific Media Corporation.

Saving Silverman

Columbia Pictures ★ Released 2001 **★ Directed by** Dennis Dugan **★ Starring** Jason Biggs, Steve Zahn, Jack Black, Amanda Peet

The cold-hearted Judith (Amanda Peet) has dug her claws into a love-struck Darren Silverman (Jason Biggs)—but his best friends Wayne Lefessier (Steve Zahn) and J.D. McNugent (Jack Black) vow to save Silverman from marrying her.

This DVD features a couple of well-hidden Easter eggs. From the main menu, select "Special Features" underneath Jason Biggs. Now scroll down and highlight the last entry on this page— "Filmographies" —but don't press Enter. Instead, tap the Right Arrow on the DVD remote and Jack Black will turn into the War Eagle mascot. Now press Enter to watch a few humorous outtakes with the giant bird suit. How do those football players keep a straight face?

When you're back to the "Special Features" menu, press the Right Arrow once again and a raccoon will appear on top of Steve Zahn's head. Press Enter to watch some funny behind-the-scenes shenanigans with the (stuffed?) raccoon hat.

Scary Movie

Dimension Films ★ Released 2000 **★ Directed by** Keenan Ivory Wayans ★
Starring Jon Abrahams, Carmen Electra, Shannon Elizabeth, Anna Faris, Kurt
Fuller, Regina Hall, Lochlyn Munro, Cheri Oteri, Dave Sheridan, Shawn Wayans,
Marlon Wayans

In this clever parody of contemporary teenage films (especially those predictable
horror flicks), a group of unsuspecting teenagers finds themselves being stalked
by a masked murderer. Sound familiar?

There's an amusing yet disturbing Easter egg for fans of the film. Watch this
film right to the end (or use the "Chapter Selection" option) and after the credits
screen, keep watching to see a funny hidden clip of Deputy Doofy Gilmore (Dave
Sheridan) and a vacuum cleaner. Not for kids!

And, while this is not exactly hidden, the *Scary Movie* DVD box doesn't tell you
that there are six "Sneak Peeks" to other DVDs such as the *Scream* Box Set, *Gone
in 60 Seconds, Hellraiser: Inferno, Don't Be a Menace to South Central while Drinking
Your Juice in the Hood*, and more. Nice surprise!

Scary Movie 2

Dimension Films ★ Released 2001 **★ Directed by** Keenan Ivory Wayans ★
Starring Shawn Wayans, Marlon Wayans, Anna Faris, Regina Hall, Christopher
Masterson, Kathleen Robertson, James Woods, Tim Curry, Tori Spelling,
Chris Elliott

In this irreverent sequel to 2000's *Scary Movie*, four teenagers are invited to spend
the night in a haunted house. Like its predecessor, this film spoofs popular
teenage horror flicks and is laced with other funny pop culture references.

Want an Easter egg? How about three? From the disc's main menu, select "Set
Up" and enter this section. Once inside, press the Up Arrow twice and an icon of
a red cat will appear on the screen. Press Enter to watch a very humorous rant
from the parrot, who complains about DVDs ("I don't want to work for my
entertainment! What's with all these menus and options?!") and the problem of
unemployed parrots ("We should bring back pirates…all of them had a parrot!
Yo ho ho, mate!").

Now, from the main menu, highlight "Bonus Material" and, once inside, enter
the subsection entitled "Alternate and Deleted Scenes." Now press the Up Arrow
once on the DVD remote (the arrow at the bottom of the screen will turn red)

and then press the Left Arrow. Another red cat will appear. Press Enter and the parrot will go on another funny rant.

But wait—there's one more…. Go back out to the main menu and select "Sneak Peeks." Once inside, scroll down to the words "Scream Trilogy" and press the Left Arrow. Another red cat will appear. Press Enter for yet another parrot rant. But there's a caveat—you'll need to wait until you hear the parrot say "Pssst…sneak peeks…yo yo yo." If he doesn't say this when you enter the "Sneak Peeks" section, exit to the main menu and re-enter until he does.

Schoolhouse Rock

Disney/Buena Vista Home Entertainment ★ Series Began 1973

This 283-minute double-disc collection includes every animated song in this educational after-school TV series for kids (and kids at heart). Who could forget "I'm Just a Bill," "Conjunction Junction, What's Your Function?" and "A Noun is a Person, Place or Thing"?! Great stuff.

Not only does this two-DVD set feature every ditty and plenty of extras, but there's a couple of Easter eggs, too. Hmm, perhaps we can sing a song about these eggs?

Here's how to access them: Pop in the first disc and from the main menu scroll down and choose "Set Up" from the list of options. Once inside, highlight the words "Main Menu"—but don't press Enter just yet. Instead, press the Right Arrow on the DVD remote and the picture of the man's face will turn red. Press Enter to access a hidden "Yohe Doodle Dandy" section, and have fun scrolling through early sketches drawn by *Schoolhouse Rock* composer and artist Tom Yohe (who passed away in 2000). This hidden area also houses a few pictures, musical clips, and early scripts, too. What a treat!

The other eggs—and there are a few of 'em—can be found on the second disc. So pop in the DVD and from the main menu select the water fountain on the right-hand side of the screen. Press Enter and the school hallway will become flooded—with a few surprise guests that appear from classic *Schoolhouse Rock* episodes.

Here's another one: Use the DVD remote to select the light switch on the left-hand side of the screen (by the sports trophy case). Press Enter and the lights will turn off. Then watch as the dancing skeleton scares off the little kids!

Last, highlight the word "Credit" on the "Extra Credit" banner hanging from the ceiling and it'll turn purple. Now press Enter and credits are what you'll get!

This launches a hidden section with credits on the making of this DVD and the *Schoolhouse Rock* episodes. There are dozens and dozens of screens to scroll through here. Wow!

Scooby-Doo

Warner Bros. Pictures ★ **Released** 2002 ★ **Directed by** Raja Gosnell ★
Starring Freddy Prinze Jr., Sarah Michelle Gellar, Matthew Lillard, Linda Cardellini, Rowan Atkinson

*Z*oinks!

The classic TV cartoon becomes a live action film—except for a computer-generated Scooby.

After years of successful sleuthing, the gang at Mystery Inc.—namely Shaggy, Velma, Fred, Daphne, and Scooby—decide to call it quits. But two years later, they each receive a cryptic invitation to Spooky Island and decide to band together once more to solve a paranormal mystery.

Want eggs? You're in luck. Pop in the disc and watch the animated main menu for a few moments. Eventually, Scooby-Doo will get scared by a monster and will drop a Scooby snack from his mouth. You can now use the DVD remote to scroll over and click on it.

Once you do, you'll be treated to a montage of on-location interview clips from the likes of Matthew Lillard (Shaggy), Linda Cardellini (Velma), first assistant director Phil Patterson, and producer Richard Suckle—who will all explain why it's not always fun to shoot a movie outdoors!

There's Something about Mary You Don't Know

- This film involves two young men fighting over a girl named Mary (page 160). Sound familiar? It should—the film *Dumb & Dumber* had the same premise—and it was also directed by the Farrelly brothers!
- Allegedly, the memorable dialogue between Mary Matthews (Cameron Diaz) and Ted Stroehmann (Ben Stiller) about there not being enough meat on a stick was originally written for an episode of *Seinfeld*. It never aired, so the Farrelly brothers bought it for use in this movie.

Serendipity

Miramax ★ Released 2001 **★ Directed by** Peter Chelsom **★ Starring** John Cusack, Kate Beckinsale, Jeremy Piven, Molly Shannon

Do you believe in fate? In this romantic comedy, Jonathan (John Cusack) and Sara (Kate Beckinsale) let destiny take control and reignite the spark kindled a few years earlier.

There's a rewarding collection of Easter eggs for those eager and savvy enough to find them. From the main menu, scroll down once and enter the "Bonus Materials" section. Once inside, highlight the words "Main Menu" (at the bottom of the screen) but don't press Enter. Instead, press the Right Arrow once on the DVD remote. A snowflake will become illuminated and you'll get kicked into a new section of extras including a storyboard comparison, theatrical trailer, an on-set diary, and more!

Shallow Hal

20th Century Fox ★ Released 2001 **★ Directed by** Bobby Farrelly, Peter Farrelly **★ Starring** Gwyneth Paltrow, Jack Black, Jason Alexander

Directed by the same brothers who brought us *There's Something About Mary* (1998) and *Me, Myself & Irene* (2000), this "heavyweight" romantic comedy stars Hal Larson (Jack Black), a shallow skirt-chaser who, after being hypnotized by a self-help guru, only sees the inner beauty of women. Of course, he doesn't realize his gorgeous girlfriend Rosemary (Gwyneth Paltrow) is actually a 300-pound woman.

From the main menu of this DVD, choose the second menu, "Language Selection," and then scroll down four times and highlight the word "English" under "Captions & Subtitles."

Don't press Enter just yet—instead, press the Right Arrow, and a blue tail will appear on Jason Alexander's shadow. Now press Enter and it'll turn red, launching a "cheeky" demonstration of the tail special effects.

Shanghai Noon

Touchstone Pictures/Buena Vista Pictures ★ Released 2000 **★ Directed by**
Tom Dey **★ Starring** Jackie Chan, Owen Wilson, Lucy Liu

East meets West in this stunt-filled Western comedy starring Jackie Chan as
a devoted Chinese Imperial Guard who travels to America to rescue a
kidnapped princess (Lucy Liu). He joins up with a laid-back cowboy, played by
Owen Wilson, on the run from the law.

From the main menu of this DVD, select "Bonus Materials" and then select
"Shanghai Surprise." Here, you'll find two fun video games that test the player's
knowledge of the film.

The payoff for finishing these games successfully is two never-before-released
clips: one is an animatic of the train crash sequence (one that didn't appear in
the film), and the other is the memorable drinking scene—but this time around
all of the Chinese spoken by Chon Wang (Chan) has English subtitles.

Showgirls

MGM ★ Released 1995 **★ Directed by** Paul Verhoeven **★ Starring** Elizabeth
Berkley, Kyle MacLachlan, Gina Gershon, Glenn Plummer, Robert Davi, Alan
Rachins

In one of the more seductively controversial Hollywood films from the
mid-'90s, Nomi Malone (Elizabeth Berkley) is determined to make it as a Las
Vegas showgirl, but in doing so, gets a good look at Sin City's seedy underbelly.

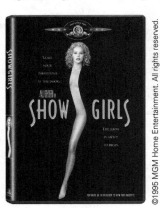

There's some extra content packed onto this
steamy DVD.

From the main menu, you'll notice an
animated showgirl sign in flashing neon lights
at the top of the screen. Each of the letters that
make up the word "Showgirls" will play a
hidden piece of dialogue from the film.

Here's how to access them: Use the Left Arrow
or Right Arrow on the remote, and scroll across
the various letters. Press Enter when on top of
one the letters such as *S* or *G* to play an audio
sound bite.

Shrek

DreamWorks Pictures ★ **Released** 2001 ★ **Directed by** Andrew Adamson, Vicky Jenson ★ **Starring** Mike Myers, Eddie Murphy, Cameron Diaz, John Lithgow

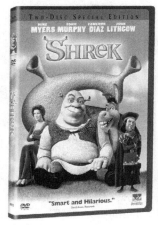

What do you get when you combine a reclusive ogre, a loudmouth donkey, a tiny-but-evil ruler, and a feisty princess with a lousy singing voice? The answer, of course, is *Shrek,* the incredibly successful computer-animated film.

As if the 11 hours of extra footage weren't enough on this two-disc set, it also contains two hidden eggs.

Pop in either of the two discs, and select the "Special Features" menu section. Now press the Up Arrow twice until the Gingerbread Man's buttons turn orange. Now press Enter to read a random *Shrek* "Fun Fact." Each time you visit this egg, you'll see a different fact.

A second egg is on the second disc. Navigate over to the word "Play," but don't press Enter just yet. Instead, press the Up Arrow and a musical note will illuminate orange. Now press Enter to view the side-splitting "Shrek in the Swamp Karaoke Dance Party." Well done!

This dance party video can also be seen simply by letting the movie roll past the credits.

The Simpsons: Season 1 Box Set

20th Century Fox ★ **Series Began** 1989 ★ **Starring** Dan Castellaneta, Julie Kavner, Nancy Cartwright, Yeardley Smith, Hank Azaria, Harry Shearer

The longest-running prime-time comedy in television history now has more than 300 episodes in the can, and this Season-One box set is a real treat for fans of the show—despite it being a little rough around the edges.

Unless you've been living under a 1974 copy of *TV Guide,* you know *The Simpsons* is an animated series starring a dysfunctional family including a lazy and slow father (Homer), a nagging homemaker (Marge), an underachiever and

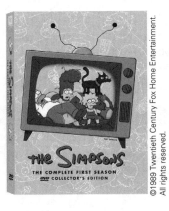

troublemaker son (Bart), a smart loner (Lisa), and a baby who doesn't talk (Maggie).

Pop in the third disc of this three-DVD box set, and head to the section "Extra Features." Now go to the second page of features by clicking the "Next" tab. Once inside, select "Art of The Simpsons," and then scroll down to the words "Extra Features"—but don't press Enter. Instead, tap the Left Arrow and Bart's comic book will change to gray. Press Enter to view a collection of magazine covers featuring America's favorite cartoon family, including *TV Guide, Newsweek,* and *Entertainment Weekly.*

Now go back to the second page of "Extra Features." Highlight the words "'Some Enchanted Evening' Script" without pressing Enter. Now tap the Left Arrow, and Bart's shirt will change from orange to purple. Press Enter to watch a humorous 1990 TV news report on Bart's alleged negative influence on kids, including profane T-shirts bearing his image and catchphrases.

The Simpsons: Season 2 Box Set

20th Century Fox ★ Series Began 1989 ★ **Starring** Dan Castellaneta, Julie Kavner, Nancy Cartwright, Yeardley Smith, Hank Azaria, Harry Shearer

Ah, who doesn't love this dysfunctional yellow family? The antics of the Simpson clan continue in this second-season box set on four DVDs.

And you bet there are a few Springfield-sized Easter eggs to find. Here's how to access them: Insert the first DVD and from the main menu enter the episode "Two Cars in Every Garage and Three Eyes on Every Fish." Once inside, enter the section entitled "Language Selection." Then press the Right Arrow three times on the DVD remote and Blinky will start to glow a radioactive green! Now press Enter to see the fish swim a special "thank you" message across the screen.

On the third disc in this set, select the "Bart's Dog Gets an F" episode from the main menu. Then select the "Language Selection" submenu. Once inside, highlight the words "Main Menu" but don't press Enter. Instead, press the Right Arrow and the bib on Santa's Little Helper will become illuminated. Now press Enter for some strange sketches of Bart and co. Press the Right Arrow on the DVD remote to access the second page.

While still on the third disc, choose the "Old Money" episode from the main menu. Once inside, highlight "Language Selection" but don't press Enter this time. Instead, press the Left Arrow on the DVD remote and Grandpa Simpson's hat will light up. Press Enter for an old (and humorous) sketch of ol' Abe!

Go back to the main menu one last time (er, on this disc, anyway) and choose the last episode on the screen, "Brush with Greatness." Now enter the "Language Selection" submenu. Once inside, press the Right Arrow on the DVD remote and the frame with Mr. Burns inside will light up. Press Enter to see some more rare sketches—this time of Mr. Montgomery C. Burns.

Now pop in the fourth disc and choose the episode entitled "Three Men and a Comic Book." Now enter the "Language Selection" submenu and highlight the words "French Dolby Surround" but don't press Enter. Instead, press the Right Arrow and the picture in the Comic Book Guy's hand will illuminate. Press Enter to see a weird sketch of Bart, Martin, and Milhouse.

Finally, go back to the main menu and select the episode entitled "Blood Feud." Now enter the "Language Selection" submenu. Once inside, highlight the words "French Dolby Surround" but don't press Enter. Instead, press the Right Arrow on the DVD remote and the statue's eye will light up. Press Enter for two pages of great sketches of Homer Simpson. Use the Right Arrow on the DVD remote to flip to the second page.

Want to Record Your Own DVD Audio Commentary?

DVDTracks.com was inspired by a Roger Ebert column entitled "You, Too, Can Be a DVD Movie Critic" (*Yahoo! Magazine*). In his column, this veteran movie critic argues that he'd like to hear what everyday movie fans who aren't being paid by the movie makers think about a feature film. So DVDTracks.com stepped in and created a site that serves as a central hub for movie fans who want to record their own audio commentary for today's DVD movies. Visitors can browse or create their own tracks that can be played back while watching a movie. Try it out for yourself at www.dvdtracks.com.

Singin' in the Rain

MGM/Warner Bros. Home Entertainment ★ **Released** 1952 ★ **Directed by** Stanley Donen, Gene Kelly ★ **Starring** Gene Kelly, Donald O'Connor, Debbie Reynolds, Jean Hagen, Millard Mitchell, Rita Moreno, Douglas Fowley, Cyd Charisse

One of the greatest Hollywood musicals ever created has two hidden eggs on its 50th-anniversary double DVD.

Here's how to access them: Pop in the first disc and from the main menu select "Special Features." Once inside, navigate over to "Reel Sound" and enter this section. Now use the DVD remote to highlight the various posters of these classic films—and press Enter over them to launch hidden video clips from each film!

Pop in the second disc and from the main menu press the Left Arrow on the DVD remote. Part of the lamppost will turn green. Now press Enter to be treated to a secret interview with award-winning director Baz Luhrman, who discusses the significance of *Singin' in the Rain*. This five-minute chat is peppered with video clips and music from the classic MGM film.

The Best TV Box Sets on DVD

It's not just movies on DVD we love—but all the beloved TV series are slowly making their way to a box set near you. Here are a dozen of the best to date:

1. The Simpsons
2. The Sopranos
3. Sex and the City
4. Friends
5. M*A*S*H
6. The X-Files
7. Star Trek: The Next Generation
8. The Complete Monty Python Flying Circus
9. Six Feet Under
10. The Family Guy
11. Roots
12. Saturday Night Live

Sister Act

Touchstone Pictures ★ Released 1992 ★ **Directed by** Emile Ardolino ★
Starring Whoopi Goldberg, Maggie Smith, Harvey Keitel

A lounge singer on the run from the mob (Whoopi Goldberg) hides out in the last place they'd look—a convent. When she's there, Sister Mary Clarence shows the other nuns how to let down their hair and have some fun.

This DVD hides a cute Easter egg. On the main menu, highlight the word "Play" (if it isn't already highlighted) but don't press Enter. Instead, press the Left Arrow on the DVD remote and one of Whoopi Goldberg's shoes will turn from red to green. Press Enter to watch actress Wendy Makkena ("Sister Mary Robert") talk about how she got the role for this film. Great anecdote!

Six Feet Under: The Complete First Season

HBO ★ Series Began 2002 ★ **Starring** Peter Krause, Michael C. Hall, Frances Conroy, Lauren Ambrose, Freddy Rodriguez, Mathew St. Patrick, Jeremy Sisto, Richard Jenkins, Rachel Griffiths

The critically acclaimed HBO TV series about a dysfunctional family who owns a funeral home is even better on DVD. The "Complete First Season" features all 13 episodes, audio commentary, a featurette, music tracks, and a deleted scene from the pilot episode.

© Home Box Office.

Pop in any of the four discs in this box set (with packaging that resembles a casket when opened!) and move the cursor over the words "Episode Index"—but don't press Enter. Instead, tap the Up Arrow and "HBO" will appear on the right side of the screen. Now press Enter to read who's responsible for this fabulous DVD box set. Menu design was created by the popular 1K Studios in North Hollywood, California.

Press Enter again to return to the main menu.

The Sixth Sense

Hollywood Pictures/Buena Vista Entertainment ★ Released 1999 ★
Directed by M. Night Shyamalan ★ **Starring** Bruce Willis, Haley Joel Osment,
Olivia Williams, Toni Collette

In this suspenseful thriller, child psychologist Dr. Malcolm Crowe (Bruce
Willis) begins to treat a young, frightened eight-year-old, Cole Sear (Haley Joel
Osment), who believes he can see dead people. Thanks to its spine-tingling twist,
The Sixth Sense became one of the most talked-about films of the past decade.

And guess what—this supernatural DVD has a little-known bonus gem.

From the disc's main menu, select the "Bonus Materials" tab, and then scroll
down all the way and select "More." You should see a jewelry box at the bottom
of this second "Bonus Materials" page. Scroll down and select it with your
remote, and the lid will open, revealing a videotape with the writing "Knight's
First Horror Film" on it.

As introduced by *The Sixth Sense* director, M. Night Shyamalan, this video was
made when he was 11 years old. The clip is about a minute and a half. Enjoy!

Snow White and the Seven Dwarfs: Platinum Edition

Walt Disney Pictures ★ Released 1937 ★ **Directed by** David Hand ★ **Starring**
Adriana Caselotti, Harry Stockwell, Lucille La Verne, Moroni Olsen, Billy Gilbert,
Pinto Colvig, Otis Harlan, Scotty Mattraw, Roy Atwell, Stuart Buchanan

Disney's revered animated masterpiece comes alive on DVD with this exhaustive
two-disc collection.

Along with the digitally restored widescreen version of the film, the discs'
special features include documentaries, galleries, games, a karaoke sing-along,
and a new rendition of "Some Day My Prince Will Come," sung by Barbara
Streisand.

A number of eggs are hidden, too.

Pop in the second ("Bonus Features") DVD, and you'll notice this main menu
screen has images representing the various sections instead of text. If you'd rather
read the names of the sections, scroll down and highlight the cauldron in the
bottom left. Now, instead of pressing Enter, press the Right Arrow and the apple
will illuminate. Press Enter to change the main menu to text options instead of
graphical ones.

Now go back to the main menu, and select the wishing-well text or image to enter the "History" and "Storyboard to Film Comparisons" submenu. Once inside the well, press the Left Arrow, and the words "DVD Credits" will appear. Press Enter to read the six pages of credits on the making of this double DVD.

And while it's not quite an egg, pop in either the first disc or the second, and don't do anything from the main menu. After awhile, the mirror will throw out random comments when he gets bored, such as "Hello, hello, is anyone home?", "Is it something I said?", or "Don't mind me—I'll just hang around 'til you decide."

The Sopranos: The Complete Second Season

HBO ★ Series Began 1999 ★ **Starring** James Gandolfini, Lorraine Bracco, Edie Falco, Michael Imperioli, Dominic Chianese, Vincent Pastore, Steve Van Zandt, Tony Sirico, Joseph Badalucco Jr., Robert Iler, Nancy Marchand, Jamie-Lynn Sigler, John Ventimiglia, Drea de Matteo, David Proval

This mega-successful HBO mob series is a raw look at the life of the fictional Mafia capo Tony Soprano, whose real family is as dysfunctional as his professional one.

A lot of time, money, and effort went into creating this DVD box set, so if you want to view the hidden production credits for *The Sopranos: The Complete Second Season,* follow these simple instructions:

Pop in any of the four discs, and from the main menu, press the Right Arrow, and a red HBO Home Video logo will appear in the bottom-right corner of the screen. Press Enter to read who's responsible for the DVD's menu design and animation, production, and audio commentary.

South Park: Volume 4

Warner Bros. ★ Series Began 1999 ★ **Developed by** Trey Parker, Matt Stone

The controversial *South Park* TV cartoon series (and feature film) chronicles the wacky adventures of four foul-mouthed boys from South Park, Colorado: Stan, Kyle, Cartman, and Kenny.

Don't be fooled by the cute appearance of these third-graders—this disc is rated MA for "Mature." That is, it has content rated not appropriate for viewers under 18 years of age.

While not quite an Easter egg, there's a hidden surprise on this fourth volume of the popular show. Instead of four episodes—as promoted on the back of the DVD box—there are actually five. And the fifth is a rare one at that.

As introduced by *South Park* creators Matt Stone and Trey Parker, the episode is entitled "Terrance and Phillip: Not Without My Anus," which aired on April Fool's Day instead of the second part of a cliff-hanger.

Six Feet Under: Some Facts

Here are a few facts about HBO's wonderful *Six Feet Under* (page 139) you may not be aware of:

- Lauren Ambrose ("Claire Fisher"), Eric Balfour ("Gabriel Dimas"), and Freddy Rodriguez ("Federico Diaz") were all in 1998's *Can't Hardly Wait*—three years before the premiere of *Six Feet Under.*
- Here's one of those continuity mistakes that some hardcore TV and movie buffs like to catch—in Season 2, Episode 5 ("The Invisible Woman"), there's a high-pitched whistle from a tea kettle. But when Ruth Fisher (played by Frances Conroy) pours water from it, there isn't a whistle on this kind of kettle.

Spaceballs

MGM ★ Released 1987 ★ **Directed by** Mel Brooks ★ **Starring** Mel Brooks, John Candy, Rick Moranis, Bill Pullman, Daphne Zuniga

O y! In this silly *Star Wars* spoof, a team of space travelers are hoping the "Schwartz" is with them as they fight off intergalactic evil.

There's an equally silly Easter egg on this DVD. Pop in the disc and from the main menu, press Enter to start the film—only when the spaceman flies across the screen and is in the middle of the target. The words "Go to Ludicrous Speed" will pop up on the screen and you'll hear Mel Brooks yell this phrase before the film begins. Cute!

Spawn

New Line Cinema ★ Released 1997 ★ **Directed by** Mark A.Z. Dippé ★ **Starring** Michael Jai White, John Leguizamo, Martin Sheen, Theresa Randle, Nicol Williamson, D.B. Sweeney

F rom the mind of comic-book legend Todd McFarlane comes this superhuman tale of good vs. evil.

Insert the "Special Features" side of the DVD. From the main menu, select "More" and then choose "Spawn Soundtrack." You will see the words "Trip Like I Do" on the left of the screen. You can use the DVD remote to highlight these words, and then press Enter to watch a Crystal Method video— but there's a cool Easter egg here too.

Highlight the words "Trip Like I Do," and then press the Right Arrow, and a picture of rocker Marilyn Manson will appear on the screen. Press Enter and a new screen with three doors will appear. Press Enter on either the right or left door, and an animated sequence will begin with creatures going out one door and in another. Do this four times and a new screen will appear with the movie's creepy clown.

Now press Enter over the middle door (with the words "Parental Advisory" on them) to launch a Marilyn Manson music video.

Remove the DVD, flip it over, and insert it. From the main menu, select the words "Scene Selections" at the bottom of the screen; instead of pressing Enter, press the Left Arrow, and the black New Line Cinema logo will turn green. Press Enter to read a "Special Thanks" screen and DVD production credits.

Speed: Five Star Collection

20th Century Fox ★ Released 1994 **★ Directed by** Jan de Bont **★ Starring** Keanu Reeves, Dennis Hopper, Sandra Bullock

In this tense action thriller, Keanu Reeves plays Officer Jack Traven, an LAPD SWAT expert who must defuse a bomb planted beneath a city bus that's set to explode if the vehicle's speed drops below 50 miles an hour. Traven is aided by one of the passengers, the gutsy Annie Porter (Sandra Bullock). Together, they must foil the efforts of a revenge-driven criminal, Howard Payne (Dennis Hopper).

Pop in the second of the two discs of this "Five Star Collection" DVD, and scroll up to the words "Action: Sequences"—but without pressing Enter just yet. Instead, tap the Left Arrow on the remote, and a small white bus will appear. Press Enter and scroll to the right a few screens until you find another bus icon. Now press Enter to watch the video clip on the "passenger-friendly" excerpt from *Speed*, in which the cargo jet explosion never occurred. This scene was omitted on the airline version of the film so it wouldn't upset passengers!

Shanghai Knights: Battle It Out!

This 2003 comedy (page 134) features the first onscreen duel between actors/martial arts experts Jackie Chan (*Rush Hour, The Tuxedo*) and Donnie Yen (*Highlander: Endgame, Blade II*), two veteran Hong Kong fighters who've never battled it out in front of the camera...until now.

Sphere

Warner Bros. Pictures ★ Released 1998 ★ **Directed** by Barry Levinson ★
Starring Dustin Hoffman, Sharon Stone, Samuel L. Jackson, Peter Coyote,
Liev Schreiber

In the depths of the Pacific Ocean lies a 300-year-old secret that may be the greatest finding in human history: a marooned spaceship. An elite underwater team of experts is assigned to find out if intelligent life still exists inside. And so the adventure begins.

Sphere is based on a Michael Crichton novel of the same name.

Pop in the disc and from the main menu scroll down and select "Reel Recommendations." Once inside, select "Actor." Now click through this section and you'll stumble upon little pink film reels for some movies. Navigate over to them and press Enter to launch trailers for the films *All the President's Men* (1976), *Sleepers* (1996), and *Above the Law* (1998).

Spider-Man

Columbia Pictures ★ Released 2002 ★ **Directed** by Sam Raimi ★ **Starring**
Tobey Maguire, Willem Dafoe, Kirsten Dunst, James Franco, Cliff Robertson,
Rosemary Harris

The Amazing Spider-Man indeed. This box office smash grossed more than $400 million at the box office in the United States alone.

Based on one of the most recognizable comic book heroes of all time, the film first reveals how geeky teenager Peter Parker (Tobey Maguire) is transformed into the web-slinging Spider-Man, and then chronicles his fight against the evil Green Goblin (Willem Dafoe). Naturally, there's a love interest too, with Parker's attractive neighbor, Mary Jane Watson (Kirsten Dunst).

There are no fewer than seven eggs hidden on the *Spider-Man* double-disc set.

Insert the first DVD and select "Special Features" from the main menu. Now choose "Commentaries." A photo of Harry Osborn (James Franco) can be seen on the left-hand side of the screen. Scroll down to "Special Features" but don't press Enter—instead, tap the Left Arrow on the DVD remote and a white spider will appear over Osborn's picture. Now press Enter to watch extensive CGI test footage and funny gags.

Go back to the "Special Features" page and this time select "Character Files." Once inside, you'll see that there are multipage biographies on the stars from the film. To access a fun secret, try the following on all but Cliff "Uncle Ben" Robertson's section: Go to the second page of each bio and press the Up Arrow on the DVD remote so that the actor's name is highlighted. Press Enter to read information on their character from the film. Take a look at the image on the screen for each—a comic-book drawing from that particular scene accompanies the shot from the film, too. Neat, huh?

All the other eggs are on the second disc. Pop it in and from the main menu go to the "The Evolution of Spider-Man" section, then select "Rogues' Gallery." Now navigate over the word "Venom" but don't press Enter. Instead, press the Down Arrow on the DVD remote and you'll see a silhouette of Spider-Man. Press Enter to see a large 3-D rendering of the character in costume. This same trick also works for Electro and Scorpion.

Now go back to the main menu and highlight the word "DVD-ROM" but don't press Enter. Instead, press the Up Arrow and a Spidey icon will appear on the screen. Now press Enter to view a hidden interview with renowned comic-book artist and toy creator Todd McFarlane.

Head back to the main menu and select "Web of Spider-Man" and then "The Evolution of Spider-Man" section. Now choose "Rogues' Gallery." Once inside, press the Up Arrow and you'll see Spider-Man's "Spidey Sense" tingling. Press Enter to view some images and information on the Sinister Six.

Lastly, go back to the main menu of disc 2 and once again select "Web of Spider-Man" and then "The Evolution of Spider-Man." Once inside, choose "Artist's Gallery." Now press the Right Arrow and the words "The Romitas" will appear in the screen. Press Enter to watch a short featurette on celebrated comic-book artists John Romita Sr. and John Romita Jr.

Spirited Away

Walt Disney Pictures ★ Released 2001 ★ **Directed by** Hayao Miyazaki ★ **Starring** (English voice actors) Daveigh Chase, Jason Marsden, Suzanne Pleshette, Michael Chiklis, Lauren Holly

In this critically acclaimed Japanese animated film, a distraught 10-year-old girl wanders away from home into a dangerous spirit world where humans are changed into animals.

This double-disc set features a fun Easter egg. Insert the first disc and from the main menu, scroll over to the right and press Enter to select the "Bonus Features" section. Once inside, press the Up Arrow on the DVD remote and these hidden words will appear in turquoise: "Meet Hayao Miyazaki." Press Enter to watch this enjoyable two-minute interview clip with the film's director, who talks about the English translation of the film. Miyazaki speaks through an interpreter and is joined by director/producer/writer John Lasseter.

Standing in the Shadows of Motown

Artisan ★ Released 2002 ★ **Directed by** Paul Justman ★ **Starring** Richard 'Pistol' Allen, Jack Ashford, Bob Babbitt, Johnny Griffith, Joe Hunter, Uriel Jones, Joe Messina, Eddie Willis, The Funk Brothers

This two-disc documentary is an inspiring look at the legendary Funk Brothers and the rise of Motown in Detroit during the late '50s.

Insert the second disc and select "More Features" from the main menu. Once inside, press the Right Arrow on the DVD remote just once and the microphone (beside the guitar) will turn red. Press Enter and enjoy a hidden two-minute rap video devoted to the Funk Brothers.

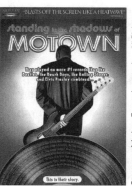

Star Trek: Deep Space Nine— The Complete First Season

Paramount Television ★ Series Began 1993 ★ **Starring** Avery Brooks, Rene Auberjonois, Nicole de Boer, Michael Dorn, Terry Farrell, Cirroc Lofton, Colm Meaney, Armin Shimerman, Alexander Siddig, Nana Visitor

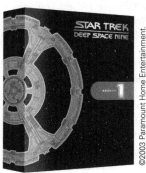

Cardassians, Klingons, and Romulans, oh my! A crew aboard Deep Space Nine (DS9) explores the outer limits of the galaxy to seek knowledge and promote peace.

The ten Easter eggs embedded in this collection are "out of this world." Pop in the last disc (disc 6) and from the main menu select "Special Features." Once inside, you'll notice that if you navigate around the DS9 space station, parts of it will illuminate in green. Press Enter to see various "Section 31" hidden files, which include character biographies of the crew members, still photos, video clips from the show, narration, and interview clips. There are ten total—can you find them all? Don't forget to go to the second page of features. Great fun for *Star Trek* buffs!

Star Trek: Deep Space Nine— The Complete Second Season

Paramount Television ★ **Series Began** 1993 ★ **Starring** Avery Brooks, Rene Auberjonois, Nicole de Boer, Michael Dorn, Terry Farrell, Cirroc Lofton, Colm Meaney, Armin Shimerman, Alexander Siddig, Nana Visitor

As with the first-season box set for this sci-fi TV series, you can find several Easter eggs by popping in the last disc (disc 7) and selecting "Special Features." Now use the DVD remote to navigate around the space station to find little objects. Press Enter over them all to see interview clips, photos, and TV show snippets about various crew members. There are a bunch to unlock—and five more secrets on the second page of extras, so be sure to look there, too.

©2003 Paramount Home Entertainment.

Star Trek—Original Series

Paramount Pictures ★ **Series Ran** 1966–1969 ★ **Starring** William Shatner, Leonard Nimoy, DeForest Kelley, James Doohan, Nichelle Nichols, George Takei, Walter Koenig

On each of the *Star Trek: The Original Series* discs, you'll find hidden TV trailers for that particular collection, and more.

Pop in the disc, and from the main menu, press the Up Arrow on the remote, and the Star Trek icon will turn from dark gray to silver. Press Enter to see four original trailers—two of which are for the episodes on that particular DVD; another two are trailers to promote the next two episodes in the series.

For example, episodes 21 and 22 (Volume 11 on DVD) will have secret trailers for episodes 21, 22, 23, and 24.

Now that's clever marketing!

Star Trek III: The Search for Spock

Paramount Pictures ★ Released 1984 ★ **Directed by** Leonard Nimoy ★ **Starring** William Shatner, Leonard Nimoy, DeForest Kelley, James Doohan, George Takei, Walter Koenig, Nichelle Nichols, Merritt Butrick, Christopher Lloyd

Admiral James T. Kirk and his trusty crew risk their careers—and perhaps their lives—stealing the U.S.S. Enterprise to recover Spock's body.

Naturally, this *Star Trek* DVD features an Easter egg that's "out of this world." Insert the second disc ("Special Features") and from the main menu, select "The Star Trek Universe" on the right-hand side of the screen. Once inside, press the Right Arrow on the DVD remote four times and the center of the object on the screen will turn white. Press Enter to watch a lengthy "making-of" featurette with Ken Ralston, the film's Supervisor of Visual Effects. He'll walk the viewer through some neat tricks of the trade. This is especially cool for Star Trek fans.

©2003 Paramount Home Entertainment.

The First DVD Board Game?

In late 2002, the first DVD Hollywood trivia board game—Scene It?—debuted. By fusing DVD technology with the old family board game, Scene It? turns the DVD player into an interactive game show host, with many motion picture and music clips, visual puzzlers, and trivia cards from famous films from studios such as MGM, Universal, DreamWorks SKG, Paramount, and Sony. For more information, visit www.sceneit.com

Star Wars: Episode I—The Phantom Menace

20th Century Fox/LucasFilm ★ Released 1999 **★ Directed by** George Lucas ★
Starring Liam Neeson, Ewan McGregor, Natalie Portman, Jake Lloyd, Ian McDiarmid

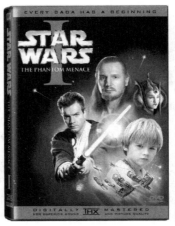

The force is back! Jedi Master Qui-Gon Jinn (Liam Neeson) and his apprentice, young Obi-Wan Kenobi (Ewan McGregor), are sent by the Chancellor of the Republic to the planet of Naboo to negotiate a heated trade dispute. The evil Senator Palpatine (and soon-to-be Emperor) is behind the strife and declares war on the innocent people of this world unless Queen "Padme Naberrie" Amidala (Natalie Portman) signs a treaty. The Queen and the annoying Nabooian creature Jar Jar Binks (Ahmed Best) are swiftly rescued by the two Jedis, but must take refuge on the planet Tatooine to find parts to repair their ship before organizing a counterattack. There they meet ten-year-old Anakin Skywalker (Jake Lloyd), a.k.a. the young Darth Vader.

There are a number of clever eggs well-hidden on the DVD release of *Star Wars: Episode I—The Phantom Menace.*

The first (and finest) egg is a blooper reel of amusing outtakes. Here's how to access it:

On the first disc, go to the "Options" menu and type "1138" using your DVD remote. (One of Lucas' early films was *THX 1138.*) On some DVD players, you might have to press 10+, 1, and then 3 and 8. Sit back and enjoy an entertaining two-minute blooper reel.

Who knew R2D2 had such problems keeping upright?

The second egg enables you to choose which of the three planet themes to get when you pop in the DVD. (The choice is random otherwise.) Once the DVD is placed into the player and the red FBI warning comes on the screen, press the number 2 to be taken to the Tatooine theme. Alternatively, press the Audio button to launch the Naboo theme, or press 10+, 2, 2 for the Coruscant theme.

Insert the second DVD of this two-disc set, and from the main menu, select "Deleted Scenes and Documentaries" in the middle of the screen. Now choose "Deleted Scenes Only"; on the next page, "Complete Podrace Grid Sequence," push the Down Arrow so that the words "Doc Menu" turn yellow. Now press the Right Arrow, and a small yellow rectangle will appear. Press Enter to watch a two-and-a-half-minute "making-of" clip for the podrace sequence.

In the same "Deleted Scenes Only" page, click the Right Arrow to enter the page entitled "Extended Podrace Lap Two." Just like before, push the Down Arrow to highlight the words "Doc Menu," and press the Right Arrow on the DVD remote. Now press Enter to watch another featurette on the making of the podrace sequence.

Star Wars: Episode II—Attack of the Clones

20th Century Fox/LucasFilm ★ Released 2002 **★ Directed by** George Lucas **★ Starring** Ewan McGregor, Natalie Portman, Hayden Christensen, Ian McDiarmid, Samuel L. Jackson, Christopher Lee

Who knew Yoda could kick butt?

Set ten years after the events of that menacing phantom, *Star Wars: Episode II—Attack of the Clones* follows the adventures of Anakin Skywalker (Hayden Christensen) and Obi-Wan Kenobi (Ewan McGregor) as they protect Senator Padmé Amidala (Natalie Portman) from a threatening faction of political separatists. A forbidden romance develops between Skywalker and Amidala, whose actions may impact the fate of the galaxy.

There are a handful of good Easter eggs on these two discs. Pop in the first DVD. From the main menu enter the "Options" screen and, once inside, press the numbers 11, then 3, and then 8 on the DVD remote (or 10+, 1, 3, and 8 on some remotes). A funny blooper reel will run through the DVD production credits. Very humorous! By the way, "1138" refers to one of George Lucas' first films, *THX 1138*.

On the second disc, choose the option that says "Dex's Kitchen and Still Galleries," second from the bottom of the screen. Now scroll down and select "To Dex's Kitchen." Once inside, highlight the words "Main Menu" but don't press Enter. Instead, press the Left Arrow once and a yellow rectangle will appear. Press Enter to view funny images from "Star Wars Want-Ads: The College Campaign." There are eight in all. Cute!

Stigmata

MGM ★ Released 1999 ★ **Directed by** Rupert Wainwright ★ **Starring** Patricia Arquette, Gabriel Byrne, Jonathan Pryce

Frankie Paige (Patricia Arquette) doesn't have faith in God. That is, until she begins to suffer the stigmata—bodily marks resembling the wounds of the crucified Christ. The Vatican's top investigator of paranormal activity, Father Kiernan (Gabriel Byrne), travels to America to see Paige and winds up in the middle of a global cover-up that could destroy the church.

The DVD contains a director's alternate ending, audio commentary, deleted scenes, a collectible eight-page booklet, trailers, videos, and an Easter egg.

From the disc's main menu, simply press the Up Arrow on the DVD remote, and a small circle above the word "Stigmata" will turn yellow. Press Enter to view a lengthy preproduction animatic of the chilling subway scene, using storyboard sketches.

Smoochy Facts

In the comedy *Death to Smoochy* (page 42), did you know that:

- Singer/actor Henry Rollins (*Johnny Mnemonic, Jack Frost*) auditioned for the role of Spinner Dunn but lost out to Michael Rispoli (*Rounders, Snake Eyes*).
- The ice skating sequence near the end of the film was choreographed and skated by Canadian idol Elvis Stojko.

Stir of Echoes

Artisan ★ Released 1999 **★ Directed by** David Koepp **★ Starring** Kevin Bacon

Tom Witzky (Kevin Bacon) doesn't believe in the supernatural, yet after he's hypnotized at a friend's party, he begins to hear and see things no one else can. Witzky soon realizes these fragmented and disturbing encounters are pieces of a puzzle he must solve… at any expense.

The eggs on this DVD aren't too hard to find but they're undocumented interview clips that are quite revealing!

From the main menu of this DVD, scroll down and press Enter over the section "Cast & Crew." Once inside, select the first entry, "Kevin Bacon," and then choose the words "Working with Kevin Bacon." A video will appear featuring actress Katherine Erbe (who plays Bacon's wife, Maggie Witzky) and director David Koepp talking about what it's like to work with Bacon on this film.

Now try the same thing with the David Koepp bio—select the entry "Working with David Koepp" to hear Bacon, Erbe, and actress Illeana Douglas (who plays Lisa in the film) chatting about the director.

Strictly Ballroom

Miramax ★ Released 1992 **★ Directed by** Baz Luhrmann **★ Starring** Paul Mercurio, Tara Morice, Bill Hunter, Pat Thomson, Gia Carides, Peter Whitford, Barry Otto

This romantic comedy is about an Australian championship ballroom dancer who is encouraged to dance his own steps by an ugly-duckling dancer, who also wants to be his partner.

This tenth anniversary DVD features audio commentary, a 3-D gallery, French and Spanish subtitles, and as a special treat, a featurette entitled "Samba To Slow Fox," an entertaining documentary that inspired *Strictly Ballroom*.

There's also a hidden egg on this DVD.

Insert the disc, and from the main menu, scroll up once and select "Sneak Peeks." Once inside this "Miramax Movies to Remember" page, press the Up

Arrow, and a white sparkle will magically appear to the right of the words "Sneak Peeks." Now press Enter to bring up a never-before-released two-minute deleted scene with Wayne (Pip Mushin), Scott (Paul Mercurio), and Fran (Tara Morice) in and outside a market.

Super Troopers

20th Century Fox ★ **Released** 2001 ★ **Directed by** Jay Chandrasekhar ★ **Starring** Jay Chandrasekhar, Kevin Heffernan, Steve Lemme, Paul Soter, Erik Stolhanske, Brian Cox, Daniel von Bargen, Marisa Coughlan, Lynda Carter

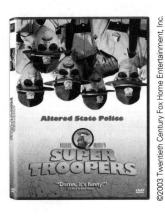

©2003 Twentieth Century Fox Home Entertainment, Inc.

Can a team of bumbling Vermont highway patrolmen solve a crime fit for the pros? This comedy answers whether these women-chasing law enforcers are duds in uniform or "super troopers."

And guess what—there's an Easter egg buried on the disc, too. From the main menu, select "Special Features" from the right-hand side of the screen. Once inside the submenu, scroll down four times until the words "Road Trip Newswrap" are highlighted. Press Enter to watch a humorous two-minute clip about the national tour to promote this film. Visit the 20th Century Fox lot in L.A. and watch the troopers stop a few drivers to question them. Very funny! But, they caution, "if you don't like it—stay off our highway!"

The Sweet Hereafter

Alliance Communications/New Line Home Entertainment ★ **Released** 1997 ★ **Directed** by Atom Egoyan ★ **Starring** Ian Holm, Maury Chaykin, Peter Donaldson, Bruce Greenwood, David Hemblen, Brooke Johnson, Arsinée Khanjian, Tom McCamus, Stephanie Morgenstern, Earl Pastko, Sarah Polley, Gabrielle Rose, Alberta Watson

This 1997 Cannes Film Festival award winner sheds light on a small, grieving town following a tragic bus accident, and on the high-profile lawyer Mitchell Stephens (Ian Holm) who promises justice and retribution. Through Egoyan's masterful storytelling, the viewer soon discovers that the community has its share of secrets, as does Stephens.

Courtesy of New Line Home Entertainment, 2003.

This "New Line Platinum Series" DVD features a handful of extra goodies and a couple of Easter eggs. In fact, music lovers will undoubtedly enjoy the eggs hidden on this disc.

Pop in the DVD and wait a few seconds. If you don't click anything, a beautiful instrumental melody from the film will play in its entirety. There are other places on this disc that feature music from the film, played in true 5.1 digital sound. Head on over to the "Special Features" page and wait a few moments for another song to play.

Want more? Take a look at the bottom of this "Special Features" screen—one of your options is to hear the film's music as an isolated score. Enjoy!

Swordfish

Warner Bros. ★ **Released** 2001 ★ **Directed by** Dominic Sena ★ **Starring** John Travolta, Hugh Jackman, Halle Berry, Don Cheadle

In this high-tech thriller, John Travolta plays a charismatic mastermind who offers $10 million to an ex-con computer hacker (Hugh Jackman) if he can break into an electronic government slush fund codenamed "Swordfish."

This DVD contains Easter eggs that *can* be accessed from a TV-based DVD player, but it may be easier to find them via a DVD-ROM drive.

Whatever your choice, start the movie and then choose Title 10. This will immediately launch an entertaining Paul Oakenfield music video for "Planet Rock (Swordfish Mix)" strewn with video clips from the film.

Next, try Titles 11 through 18 to access various hidden interview snippets with the cast and crew. (You'll know you've found the eggs when the screen flashes "Password Accepted.")

Title 19 will show a slideshow of preproduction color sketches from *Swordfish*.

The Terminator: Special Edition

MGM ★ Released 1984 **★ Directed by** James Cameron **★ Starring** Arnold Schwarzenegger, Michael Biehn, Linda Hamilton

In the near future, computers dominate the planet and are bent on exterminating the human race once and for all. To ensure their success, the machines send a seemingly indestructible cyborg (Arnold Schwarzenegger) back in time to kill Sarah Connor (Linda Hamilton), whose unborn son could become mankind's only hope.

Fans of James Cameron's big-budget flick will undoubtedly get a kick out of the many hidden eggs on this rerelease of the film.

Pop in the side of the disc that says "Widescreen," and from the main menu, enter the section entitled "Special Features." Once inside, press the Down Arrow on the remote three times. A small square at the top of the screen will turn green. Press Enter to watch four randomly generated featurettes on the making of the movie.

Another well-hidden collection of five featurettes can be uncovered in the "Languages" section of the DVD. Scroll down to highlight "Français" (under the "Spoken Languages" menu), but instead of pressing Enter, press the Right Arrow, and a box will turn green on the right side of the screen. Press Enter for one of five randomly generated featurettes.

And there's more: Enter the "Scene Selections" area from the main menu, and select "Chapters 13–16," but don't press Enter. Now press the Down Arrow twice to highlight another box at the top of the screen. Press Enter to watch a randomly generated interview segment. There are five.

While still here in the "Scene Selections" area, try the same thing in "Chapters 25–28" and "Chapters 29–32" for more hidden goodies.

T2—Extreme DVD

Artisan ★ Released 1991 ★ **Directed by** James Cameron ★ **Starring** Arnold Schwarzenegger, Linda Hamilton, Edward Furlong, Robert Patrick

He said he'd be back! Arnold returns in this DVD re-release of the action sci-fi flick *Terminator 2: Judgment Day*— but with superior video and audio quality, extra features, and, of course, Easter eggs!

Here's how to access them: Pop in the first disc and from the main menu highlight the words "Sensory Control" but don't press Enter. Instead, press the Right Arrow on the DVD remote five times. Now the words "The Future Is Not Set" will appear on the right-hand side of the screen. Now press Enter and the terminator will morph, confirming that you've accessed the egg. What is it? You'll see the words "Play Theatrical Version" change next to "Play Special Edition" of the film—with many extra scenes!

Now pop in the second disc and, from the main menu, highlight the "DVD-ROM" option at the bottom of the screen but don't press Enter. Instead, press the Left Arrow on the DVD remote and the symbol in the lower left-hand corner of the screen will illuminate. Press Enter to watch a hidden two-minute trailer for the earlier "T2: Ultimate Edition DVD" from Artisan, including scenes from the movie, menus, and extra content. Very cool.

Wait—there's one more. From the main menu of this second disc, highlight the option that says "High Definition" but don't press Enter just yet. Instead, press the Up Arrow on the DVD remote and a half-circle will appear on the symbol in the top right of the screen. Press Enter now to see production credits for this two-disc set.

Did You Know?

Lance Henriksen (*Aliens, The Right Stuff,* the *Millennium* TV series) was originally cast as the Terminator, and Arnold Schwarzenegger as the good guy—but when "Ah-nold" read the script, he asked to play the big T.

Apparently, the infamous O.J. Simpson was considered for the role of the Terminator, but the producers were concerned the ex-football star wouldn't be taken seriously. Ahem.

Terminator 2: Judgment Day (T2: The Ultimate Edition DVD)

Artisan ★ Released 1991 **★ Directed by** James Cameron **★ Starring** Arnold Schwarzenegger, Linda Hamilton, Edward Furlong, Robert Patrick

Schwarzenegger promised he'd be back, and here he is reprising his role as a T-800 "Terminator." But this time he's been sent back to protect young John Connor (Edward Furlong) and his mother, Sarah (Linda Hamilton), instead of killing them. But a more advanced cyborg (played by Robert Patrick) with shape-shifting abilities also heads back in time to kill Connor before he can grow up to lead the resistance against machines.

Along with the original theatrical version of *Terminator 2: Judgment Day* and the "Special Edition" DVD version, there is a third, undocumented version of the film—planted as an Easter egg.

Pop in the disc with the movie side up (it says "Side A" on the inner rim), and from the main menu, scroll down to select "Special Edition." This will open up a few more menu options, and you'll notice there are five odd-looking roman numerals along the right side of the screen.

Here's what to do:

Using your DVD remote, type 8, 2, 9, 9, and 7, which happens to be the date of "judgment day" as prophesized in the film (August 29, 1997). The five symbols along the right side of the screen will spell "The Future Is Not Set" in yellow.

Now press Enter to watch the "Extended Special Edition" of the feature film with extra scenes and an alternate ending. This exciting version is 156 minutes long, and needless to say, a real treat for fans of this sci-fi series.

If accessing this hidden movie is too tough for you, simply start watching any of the two versions, and access Title 3 using your DVD remote to launch this third version.

There are more goodies buried on this DVD. Take out the disc and flip it over to play "Side B" with all the special features on it. At the main menu, do not select from any of these three options; after a half-minute or so, one of three random events will happen:

- The face of a T-1000 will morph out of the center of the screen and tell you to "Get Out!"
- A TV screen will appear and flicker on the bottom-left corner of the screen with the words "Join the Resistance." If you click on it fast enough, it'll take you to a hidden screen "written" by Connor, telling you about a secret place to go online to train for the upcoming war.
- The same TV screen will show snow again (but without the words "Join the Resistance"). Press Enter and the face of Beethoven will be seen in space, breaking open to reveal the Terminator's face. This is a short "Swelltone" trailer.

Coolest-Looking DVD Boxes

Evil Dead: Book of the Dead Edition has a rubber/foam casing designed to resemble the book of the dead from the film.

Basic Instinct: Special Edition features a see-through plastic case that looks like a block of ice—and inside is a pen that resembles an ice pick.

The DVD case for *Total Recall: Special Edition* is a round red tin with bumps that resembles the planet Mars.

Terminator 2: Ultimate Edition, T2—Extreme DVD, the *Rambo* box set, and *Highlander: Ultimate Edition* feature a cool metallic casing.

Courtesy of Artisan Home Entertainment Inc.

Courtesy of Artisan Home Entertainment Inc.

There's Something about Mary

20th Century Fox ★ Released 1998 **★ Directed by** Peter Farrelly, Bobby Farrelly
★ Starring Cameron Diaz, Matt Dillon, Ben Stiller, Lee Evans, Chris Elliot

Even geeks deserve a second chance. That's the premise behind this outrageous comedy in which the nerdy Ted (Ben Stiller) is still in love with his high school crush, Mary (Cameron Diaz). In order to track her down, Ted hires a sleazy P.I. (Matt Dillon), who also falls in love with her.

There's Something about Mary still holds the record for the most disgustingly funny scene in any comedy flick to date.

Pop in the disc, and from the main menu press the Right Arrow four times until Mary's red dress turns turquoise. Now press Enter to read the credits for this DVD. B1 Media is responsible for the disc's animation, menu interface, and audio effects.

This little-known egg works on both the regular DVD and the "Special Edition" version that features extra footage and a karaoke music video.

The Thing: Collector's Edition

Universal Studios ★ Released 1982 **★ Directed by** John Carpenter **★ Starring** Kurt Russell

A deadly alien is awakened from a 100,000-year deep freeze under the Earth's crust and is not too happy about it. An American research team working in the Antarctic tundra is determined to put an end to its wrath, but discovers the creature's ability to morph into other living beings, making it difficult to tell who is human and who is not.

Universal Studios has placed an unannounced feature on this creepy DVD.

From the main menu, select "Bonus Materials" and then choose the "Terror Takes Shape" documentary. From the three options ("Chapter List," "Language Selection," and "Play"), choose "Language Selection," and you will find the entry "Music Score." Once this is selected (by pressing Enter over it), choose the words "Play Movie" to watch the entire documentary—but with just the musical score!

Three Kings

Warner Bros. ★ **Released** 1999 ★ **Directed by** David O. Russell ★ **Starring** George Clooney, Mark Wahlberg, Ice Cube, Spike Jonze

This dark comedy takes place during the Gulf War, when four American soldiers search for stolen Kuwaiti gold in the Iraqi desert and are followed by a nosy reporter looking for a story. In the end, the team finds something much more valuable.

From the disc's main menu, select "Special Features" and then choose "Production Notes" near the bottom of the screen. Now select the first entry, "Origins." Once inside, press the Up Arrow on the remote, and a red grenade will appear. Press Enter to watch an entertaining TV spot for *Three Kings*.

Next, go back to the main menu, and select "Special Features" and then the first option, "Cast & Crew." Press the Up Arrow, and another red grenade will appear. Press Enter and take note of this secret code: "SCUD." This is to be used on the *Three Kings* Events web site, accessible through the DVD-ROM portion of the disc. A treasure awaits you if you succeed!

The second password can be found once again in the "Special Features" section of the DVD, but choose the word "Continue" to go to the second, and then third page of features. Now press the Down Arrow on the remote until another red grenade appears. This web site password is "BAGHDAD."

The Tigger Movie

Walt Disney Pictures ★ **Released** 2000 ★ **Directed by** Jun Falkenstein ★ **Starring** John Hurt, Jim Cummings, Nikita Hopkins, Ken Sansom, John Fiedler, Peter Cullen, Andre Stojka, Kath Soucie, Tom Attenborough

In this animated tale of friendship, love, and family, a scheme by Tigger's friends— including Winnie the Pooh, Roo, Piglet, Eeyore, Rabbit, and Owl—backfires as they try to cure Tigger's loneliness.

From the main menu, enter the "Bonus Materials" section, and the first entry will be a "Tigger Movie Trivia Game." Select it and if you answer all of the questions correctly, it'll unlock a secret "video prize" discussing the history of Winnie the Pooh including the stuffed animals that inspired the characters, how Walt Disney heard about them, and much more.

If you're having difficulty answering all the multiple-choice questions, select Title 5 on your DVD remote (or by using DVD-ROM software on a computer).

Titus

20th Century Fox ★ **Released** 1999 ★ **Directed by** Julie Taymor ★ **Starring** Sir Anthony Hopkins, Jessica Lange, Alan Cumming, Harry Lennix, Jonathan Rhys Meyers, Angus Macfadyen

Based on the Shakespeare play *Titus Andronicus*, this film adaptation by Broadway director Julie Taymor is a dark and often disturbing drama about an aging Roman general, Titus (Sir Anthony Hopkins), who returns home from war against the Goths with the Gothic queen, Tamora (Jessica Lange), and her two sons.

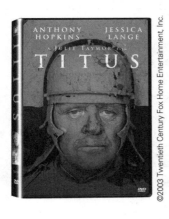

Pop in the second DVD (the one with the picture of Tamora on the disc) and from the main menu, highlight the words "Making of Titus" but don't press Enter. Instead, tap the Right Arrow on the DVD remote and a bright yellow helmet will appear over the animal face. Press Enter to read the full credits for the making of this two-disc DVD collection. The popular 1K Studios was responsible for the disc's menu design and animation.

Did You Know?

Released in 1995, *Toy Story* (page 164) was the first full-length computer-animated movie.

Tombstone: Vista Series

Hollywood Pictures/Buena Vista Pictures ★ Released 1993 ★ **Directed by** George P. Cosmatos ★ **Starring** Kurt Russell, Val Kilmer, Michael Biehn, Powers Boothe, Robert Burke, Dana Delany, Sam Elliott, Stephen Lang, Joanna Pacula, Bill Paxton, Jason Priestley, Michael Rooker, Jon Tenney, Billy Zane, Charlton Heston

The "Vista Series" director's cut of this popular Western chronicles the action-packed, real-life family feud between the Earps and the Clantons.

The Easter egg on this double-disc set is worth finding for fans of the film. Pop in the second DVD and, from the main menu, press the Right Arrow on the DVD remote. A yellow sheriff's badge will appear in the lower right-hand corner of the screen. Press Enter to view an impressive image gallery of rare posters, set designs, and sketches from this feature film. There are 36 in all. How neat!

Top Secret!

Paramount Pictures ★ Released 1984 ★ **Directed by** Jim Abrahams, David Zucker, Jerry Zucker ★ **Starring** Val Kilmer, Lucy Gutteridge

This slapstick comedy, in the same vein as *Airplane!* and *The Naked Gun*, stars Val Kilmer as American rock star Nick Rivers, who falls in love with Hillary Flammond (Lucy Gutteridge), the daughter of a brilliant but dangerous German scientist. Essentially, this flick is a silly parody of Elvis films and war epics.

©2003 Paramount Home Entertainment.

From the main menu, scroll down to "Special Features" and click on it. Now select "Storyboards" to enter this area. Once inside, scroll down three times until the words "Special Features" are highlighted—but don't press Enter. Instead, press the Right Arrow on the remote and the eye in the magnifying glass will turn yellow. Now press Enter to watch the original footage used for the hilarious Swedish bookstore scene—you'll notice that it's not played in reverse as in the film!

Total Recall: Special Limited Edition

Artisan Entertainment ★ **Released** 1990 ★ **Directed by** Paul Verhoeven ★ **Starring** Arnold Schwarzenegger

"They stole his mind, now he wants it back" was the tagline for this sci-fi thriller with incredible special effects. In the near future, construction worker Douglas Quaid (Arnold Schwarzenegger) takes a "virtual vacation" on the planet Mars, but when he awakens, finds his friends and family are trying to kill him. Quaid takes a real trip to Mars to unravel an "out of this world" conspiracy.

Courtesy of Artisan Home Entertainment Inc.

This cool-looking limited edition DVD—packaged in a round tin designed to look like Mars—features a small Easter egg…if you know where to look.

From the disc's main menu, select the "Setup" tab (second from the bottom). Press Enter to be taken to another menu screen, and scroll down to highlight the words "Main Menu" at the bottom of the screen. Now press the Left Arrow on the remote twice, and the red JVC logo in the corner of the screen will turn white.

Press Enter to view a commercial for JVC products.

Toy Story: The Ultimate Toy Box

Walt Disney Pictures/Pixar Animation Studios ★ **Released** 1995 *(Toy Story)*, 1999 *(Toy Story 2)* ★ **Directed by** John Lasseter *(Toy Story)*; John Lasseter, Ash Brannon, Lee Unkrich *(Toy Story 2)* ★ **Starring** Tom Hanks, Tim Allen, Joan Cusack, Kelsey Grammer, Don Rickles, Jim Varney, Wallace Shawn, John Ratzenberger, Annie Potts

Disney/Pixar's computer-animated feature films are a peek into the (mis)adventures of a child's toys, including the antics of a popular spaceman toy named Buzz Lightyear (Tim Allen) and a cowboy, Sheriff Woody (Tom Hanks).

This "Ultimate Toy Box" box set offers hours of bonus features—but there are also some hidden goodies worth finding, too.

Insert disc 3 and choose *Toy Story 2*. Then select "Jesse's Song" in the "Story" section and press the Left Arrow. A question mark will appear on the screen— press Enter to watch a funny outtake by two of the film's directors, Ash Brannon and John Lasseter.

Also on the same disc, select *Toy Story 2*, and then enter the "History" area. Now click on "The Continuing World of Toy Story. " After this short video clip ends (or once you skip to the next frame), there's a hidden menu entitled "Links." Press Enter. This bonus screen houses many other new features to kick back and watch, such as abandoned reels from Woody's Nightmare and Buzz Lightyear's cartoon.

Treasure Planet

Walt Disney Pictures ★ Released 2002 ★ **Directed by** Ron Clements, John Musker ★ **Starring** Joseph Gordon-Levitt, John Rzeznik, Brian Murray, David Hyde Pierce, Martin Short, Emma Thompson, Roscoe Lee Browne, Michael Wincott, Patrick McGoohan, Laurie Metcalf

The classic *Treasure Island* gets an animated spin as deep space replaces the high seas in this swashbuckling adventure.

There are a couple of Easter eggs to unlock—should you be able to find them. OK, we'll help you out: Pop in the DVD, and from the main menu select the "Set Up" menu entry from the list of options. Once inside, press the Right Arrow on the DVD remote and a movie clapboard will appear. Press Enter and it'll turn red before the DVD launches into three pages of credits acknowledging those who worked on the disc's supplemental material, DVD menus, design, 3-D animation, authoring, and compression.

Also from the main menu, select "Bonus Materials" and then select "Intergalactic Space Adventures." Once inside, choose the first option, "RLS Legacy: Virtual 3D Tour and Treasure Hunt." Play this treasure hunt game and find all eight map spheres. (Listen to the instructions carefully!) If you find them all, you can unlock an alternate version of a classic scene from the film. Enjoy!

Tron: Collector's Edition

Walt Disney Pictures ★ **Released** 1982 ★ **Directed by** Steven Lisberger ★
Starring Jeff Bridges, Bruce Boxleitner, David Warner, Cindy Morgan,
Barnard Hughes

In this groundbreaking special effects extravaganza, Kevin Flynn (Jeff Bridges) is a hacker who breaks into an ex-employer's computer system to prove they stole his programs, when he finds himself beamed inside of the mainframe. Flynn must fight for his life in a number of gladiator games and find a way to get back to reality.

Insert the second disc and stay on the animated main menu without touching any of the buttons on your DVD remote. Eventually "www.tronkillerapp.com" appears on the screen. If you type that web address into your Internet browser, it'll take you to a secret site.

Also on this second DVD, select "Publicity" on the bottom right of the main menu. Once inside, scroll down to highlight the words "Publicity and Merchandising," but don't press Enter just yet. Instead, press the Down Arrow one more time, and the red words "DVD Credits" will appear on the left of the screen. Press Enter to read who's responsible for this two-disc DVD set.

12 Monkeys

Universal Pictures ★ **Released** 1995 ★ **Directed by** Terry Gilliam ★ **Starring**
Bruce Willis, Madeline Stowe, Brad Pitt, Christopher Plummer

This underrated sci-fi thriller tells of a future in which the world's population is devastated by a deadly virus. James Cole (Bruce Willis) travels back in time to obtain a pure virus sample to help scientists develop a cure in the future. But Cole is institutionalized in a mental health facility, where he meets a beautiful psychiatrist (Madeline Stowe) and a troubled patient (Brad Pitt).

There's a small egg on this DVD that's fairly easy to find. From the main menu, scroll down to select "Bonus Materials." Once inside, navigate down to enter the section entitled "Cast & Filmmakers." Buried inside director Terry Gilliam's section is a hidden trailer to his 1998 flick *Fear and Loathing in Las Vegas*. Click on it to start the preview.

The Twilight Zone—Vol. 28 to 43

Image Entertainment ★ Series Ran 1959–1964 **★ Created by** Rod Serling

Created by visionary writer Rod Serling, the original *Twilight Zone* TV series on CBS (156 episodes in total) proved to be one of the most influential science fiction shows in television history. Tales about aliens, robots, monsters, and magic were cleverly disguised social commentaries about human life in the 20th century.

View any of the *Twilight Zone* DVDs from Image Entertainment (Volumes 28 through 43), and you can unlock an Easter egg within.

From the main menu, click the Right Arrow on the DVD remote once to highlight "Inside the Twilight Zone." Press Enter and then choose the last entry, "Reviews and Credits."

Now you should see a listing of the four episodes on the DVD. On at least two of them, you can select the episode and press the Right Arrow, which will launch a gray star. Press Enter to be taken to the musical score from that particular episode.

Back in the "Reviews and Credits" page, this time press the Right Arrow twice over your favorite episode, and press Enter to view original product placements and program bumpers from that episode.

Twin Peaks: Fire Walk with Me

New Line Cinema ★ Released 1992 **★ Directed by** David Lynch **★ Starring** Sheryl Lee, Moira Kelly, David Bowie, Chris Isaak, Harry Dean Stanton, Ray Wise, Kyle MacLachlan, Kiefer Sutherland

Serving as a prequel to the unconventional *Twin Peaks* TV series, *Twin Peaks: Fire Walk with Me*—the film—follows two FBI agents determined to unravel a murder mystery in the town of Twin Peaks, a place where nothing is as it seems.

That David Lynch is one weird dude. So it's no surprise that the Easter egg on this DVD is, too. From the main menu, scroll down three times until the white New Line logo is selected at the bottom of the screen. Press Enter and watch the credits roll—but take a look at the background image. It's an extreme close-up of someone eating corn by the spoonful. When the credits are over, this video clip continues to loop.

Er, talk about a conversation piece for when the company arrives! Downright freaky.

Twin Peaks—Season One Box Set

Artisan ★ **Series Ran** 1990–1991 ★ **Starring** Kyle MacLachlan

From the minds of Mark Frost and David Lynch came *Twin Peaks,* a wildly imaginative and critically acclaimed TV drama from the early '90s.

The first-season box set features a number of extras—including two Easter eggs on each of the four DVDs.

Pop in any of the discs, and from the main menu, select any episode by scrolling right or left and pressing Enter. Once inside the new screen, select "Episode Features" and then press the Up Arrow. A beige flame will appear in the upper-left corner of the screen. Press Enter to view secret interview clips.

Here's the breakdown of what you'll find, by episode:

- Disc 1, Episode 1: An interview snippet with director Duwayne Dunham
- Disc 1, Episode 2: An interview snippet with series director of photography Frank Byers
- Disc 2, Episode 3: An interview snippet with director Tina Rathborne (with her son and guinea pig!)
- Disc 2, Episode 4: An interview snippet with director Tim Hunter
- Disc 3, Episode 5: An interview snippet with director Lesli Linka Glatter
- Disc 3, Episode 6: An interview snippet with director Caleb Deschanel
- Disc 4, Episode 7: An interview snippet with series production designer Richard Hoover
- Disc 4, "Tibet" Section: A hidden DVD-credits screen with 14 pages of text and pictures

Also, while on the DVD Credits page that begins "Special Thanks from Three-Legged Cat," press the Up Arrow and a flame will appear on the right. Press Enter to view a scary (and silly) video entitled "Spencer's Rock," featuring actor Michael Anderson from the *Twin Peaks* series.

U.S. Marshals: Special Edition

Warner Bros. ★ **Released** 1998 ★ **Directed by** Stuart Baird ★ **Starring** Tommy Lee Jones, Wesley Snipes, Robert Downey Jr.

Oscar-winning Tommy Lee Jones returns as Chief Deputy Samuel Gerard (from 1993's *The Fugitive*), a U.S. Marshal determined to capture Mark Sheridan (Wesley Snipes), an accused murderer, who escapes a devastating plane crash en route to prison. In his manhunt, Gerard is joined by other agents, including John Royce (Robert Downey Jr.).

Trailer fanatics should enjoy the two hidden ones planted on this "Special Edition" DVD.

Insert the side of the disc labeled "Special Features," and from the main menu, scroll down, press Enter over the words "Special Features," and then choose "Fugitive Files."

Now select "History of the U.S. Marshals"—at the end of this featurette will be two secret movie trailers: one for 1994's *Wyatt Earp* and the other for 1973's *Cahill U.S. Marshal.*

Unbreakable

Touchstone Pictures/Buena Vista Pictures ★ **Released** 2000 ★ **Directed by** M. Night Shyamalan ★ **Starring** Bruce Willis, Samuel L. Jackson

In this suspenseful supernatural thriller, David Dunn (Bruce Willis) awakens from a deadly train crash as the sole survivor and meets a mysterious stranger, Elijah Price (Samuel L. Jackson), who believes comic-book heroes walk the Earth.

This little-known DVD feature will work on either disc in the double-DVD "Vista Series" package.

From the main menu, watch as pieces of key dialogue from the film scroll from right to left. On disc 1, it'll be lines from Dunn(Willis), and disc 2 is of Price (Jackson).

But if you don't touch any of the buttons on the DVD remote, you'll begin to hear the dialogue spoken by the characters instead of just seeing the text fly by.

Undercover Brother

Universal Pictures ★ Released 2002 ★ **Directed by** Malcolm D. Lee ★
Starring Eddie Griffin, Chris Kattan, Denise Richards, Dave Chapelle, Aunjanue
Ellis, Neil Patrick Harris, Chi McBride, Billy Dee Williams

This hilarious spoof stars Eddie Griffin as a kung-fu-fighting, Afro-wearing secret agent who uses his slick gadgets, gushy charm, and Caddy convertible to uncover a conspiracy to brainwash humanity. Who's responsible? "The Man," of course.

©2003 Universal Studios Home Video.

There are a handful of funny famous quotes from this film in three separate areas. First, go to "Scenes" (scene selection) and once inside, press the Up Arrow and then the Left Arrow. The yellow letters "UB" will appear on the screen. Press Enter to read some silly quotes from the film, such as, "Once you've had Undercover Brother, there is no other."

Go back out to the main menu. More quotes are found in the "Languages" section. Enter this area from the main menu and, once inside, scroll down to highlight the word "Espanol"—but don't press Enter. Instead, press the Left Arrow and the letters "UB" will appear. Press Enter for more.

Lastly, enter the "Bonus Materials" area. On the first page navigate over to the first option, "Alternate Ending," and use the DVD remote to highlight the word "On." Now press the Down Arrow and the "UB" letters will appear again. Press Enter and enjoy.

Did You Know?

In *Unbreakable* (page 169), the character Elijah Price (played by Samuel L. Jackson) says he's called "Mr. Glass" for his brittle physical condition. There are many ways the filmmaker visually reinforces this:

- Price's cane is made of glass.
- He's seen in many reflections such as in mirrors, a TV screen, and a glass picture frame in his art gallery.
- He leaves his card on David Dunn's windshield.

Urban Legend

Columbia TriStar ★ Released 1998 ★ **Directed by** Jamie Blanks ★ **Starring**
Jared Leto, Alicia Witt, Rebecca Gayheart, Joshua Jackson, Loretta Devine, Tara
Reid, Michael Rosenbaum, Robert Englund

Beautiful New England college student
Natalie Simon (Alicia Witt) believes that
a series of killings is related to urban legends.

From the main menu of this DVD, scroll
down and enter the "Special Features"
section. Select the "Making of" featurette and
watch it to the end (or fast-forward through
it). After the post-production music section.
the director will introduce a deleted sex scene
with Parker (Michael Rosenbaum) and Sasha
(Tara Reid) that never made it to the film.
The commentary explains what the scene is
about and why it was ultimately deleted.
Warning: Not for young eyes.

The Usual Suspects: Special Edition

MGM ★ Released 1995 ★ **Directed by** Bryan Singer ★ **Starring** Gabriel Byrne,
Kevin Spacey, Stephen Baldwin, Chazz Palminteri, Pete Postlethwaite, Kevin Pollak

In this award-winning film, five small-time crooks are rounded up as suspects.

"You think you can catch Keyser Soze?"

This "Special Edition" DVD is loaded with
features including four featurettes, a gag reel
of bloopers, deleted scenes, audio
commentary, and more.

To access the Easter eggs, pop the disc in
the player with the "Special Features" side
facing up. From the animated main menu,
press the Up Arrow, and the words "The
Usual Suspects" will illuminate in yellow.
Press Enter.

This will now take you to a secret menu screen on the DVD with a handful of items that can be selected by pressing the four arrow keys. If you choose the correct items in the proper order, you will unlock two additional featurettes on the DVD—one is an interview with a film historian and John Ottman, the person responsible for the music in the film, and the other is some interview outtakes.

The correct sequence is "Quartet," "Guatemala," then the lady, and finally, the broken cup.

National Lampoon's Van Wilder—The Unrated Version

Artisan ★ Released 2002 ★ **Directed by** Walt Becker ★ **Starring** Ryan Reynolds, Tara Reid, Tim Matheson, Paul Gleason

This *Animal House*-esque adult comedy follows the antics of Van Wilder (Ryan Reynolds), a seventh-year college student with no plans to graduate, and Gwen Pearson (Tara Reid), a sexy on-campus reporter out to expose the truth about Van's "wilder" side.

There are a handful of Easter eggs on this "unrated" disc, many of which contain nudity, so be forewarned. Actually, this double DVD set may be the first to offer Easter eggs in both a "censored" and an "uncensored" version—you choose.

From the main menu, press the Up Arrow on the DVD remote twice and a yellow star will appear in the middle of the young woman's T-shirt (over the movie's name). Press Enter to see a girl dancing with the words "Me Likey!" on her shirt.

Now go back to the main menu and press the "Setup" button to enter that section. Once inside, press the Up Arrow once and a black star will appear—but don't press Enter. Instead, press the Down Arrow and the star will turn pink. Then press the Up Arrow one last time and it'll turn yellow. Now press Enter to see the girl dancing again, this time with a recipe for a "Naked Martini" on her T-shirt.

For the uncensored version of this same clip, go back to the main menu and select the icon on the left-hand side that says "View Movie Uncensored." Now follow the same instructions as before (for both Easter eggs) and the girl's T-shirt will mysteriously turn very wet this time around. Also, while you are accessing the "Setup" screen, the girl will remove her T-shirt completely before putting on another T-shirt with the audio options.

Having fun? Wait—there's more. Now pop in the second DVD and, from the main menu, highlight the words "Van Wilder Files" on the left-hand side of the screen but don't press Enter. Instead, press the Up Arrow and a yellow star will appear on the *d* in the word "Unrated." Now press the Up Arrow three more times (the star will turn pink, then yellow, then pink again) and press Enter to see the girl dancing again with the words "Party Girl" on her shirt. It's the ingredients and instructions for another drink recipe.

Now go back to the main menu and go to the second page of features. Highlight the words "Reel Comedy" on the right-hand side of the girl's shirt, but don't press Enter. Instead, Press the Up Arrow and a yellow star will appear over the words "Van Wilder." Now press the Down Arrow, then Up, and then Down again (the star will turn white, then yellow, then white again). Now press Enter to see the girl dancing with another recipe on her shirt, this time entitled "Pink Panties."

The "uncensored" versions of the Easter eggs on disc 2 can be accessed by first selecting the "View Movie Uncensored" icon on the left of the main menu. After pressing Enter over this icon, press the Left Arrow and a little yellow finger will now appear in the top right of the screen. Now press the Right Arrow and then the Left Arrow again (the finger will turn to pink and back to yellow again) and now press Enter. The girl will flash her breasts once again. (Isn't she getting cold?)

Go back to the main menu and highlight the words "Van Wilder Files." Now press the Up Arrow, then the Down Arrow, then the Up Arrow, and then the Down Arrow again, and then press Enter when the star turns pink. The egg? A bouncing girl in a wet Van Wilder T-shirt. Surprise, surprise.

There's more—go to the second page of the main menu and highlight the words "Reel Comedy." Press the Up Arrow and a yellow star will appear over the words "Van Wilder." Now press the Down Arrow, then Up, then Down again. (The star will turn white, then yellow, then white again.) Now press Enter to see the "DVD Authoring Dude" dancing in a wet T-shirt! Hilarious! Didn't expect that, did you?

Did You Know?

Penélope Cruz also starred as Sofia Serrano in the original Spanish version of "Vanilla Sky," entitled "Abre los ojos" ("Open Your Eyes"), directed by Alejandro Amenábar in 1997.

Vanilla Sky

Paramount Pictures ★ Released 2001 ★ **Directed by** Cameron Crowe ★
Starring Tom Cruise, Penélope Cruz, Kurt Russell, Jason Lee, Noah Taylor,
Cameron Diaz

David Aames (Tom Cruise) has it all—fame, fortune, youth, good looks, and a woman he loves (Penélope Cruz)—but it all comes crumbling down in a fateful encounter with a jealous lover (Cameron Diaz). The viewer is taken on a rollercoaster ride, continually guessing what's real and what's not.

From the main menu of this DVD, head over to the "Special Features" section and then choose "Photo Galleries." Once inside, scroll up to the words "Special Features," but don't press Enter. Instead, tap the Right Arrow on the DVD remote, and the white mask on the right side of the screen will turn pink.

Now press Enter to view over five minutes of deleted scenes, outtakes, and bloopers.

Vertigo: Collector's Edition

Universal Pictures ★ Released 1958 ★ **Directed by** Alfred Hitchcock ★
Starring James Stewart, Kim Novak, Barbara Bel Geddes, Tom Helmore,
Henry Jones

The only thing better than curling up with a Hitchcock video on a lazy Sunday afternoon is when it's on DVD—and restored beautifully.

Set in San Francisco, this classic thriller begins as detective Scottie Ferguson (James Stewart) is hired to follow a friend's suicidal wife, Madeline (Kim Novak). But business soon turns personal as he falls in love with the mysterious beauty—before she dies. And so the plot-twisting adventure begins.

There's a fantastic Easter egg on this disc. From the main menu, select "Bonus Materials"

©2003 Universal Studios Home Video.

and then click on the first entry to watch the lengthy must-see documentary, "Obsessed with Vertigo: New Life for Hitchcock's Masterpiece." When it's over (you can either watch it or fast-forward to fast-track), you'll be treated to a couple of trailers for *Vertigo* (the original and the restored versions) and, as a special treat for Hitchcock fans, a two-minute deleted scene from the film!

Village of the Damned

Universal Pictures ★ Released 1995 ★ **Directed by** John Carpenter ★
Starring Christopher Reeve, Kirstie Alley, Linda Kozlowski, Michael Paré

John Carpenter's chilling remake of this classic 1960 flick follows a strange force that takes over a peaceful coastal town, prompting ten women to mysteriously become pregnant— and simultaneously give birth. The offspring are anything but ordinary.

©2003 Universal Studios Home Video.

Fans of movie trailers will enjoy the many littered throughout this DVD. From the main menu, scroll down and select "Bonus Materials" and then select "Cast and Filmmakers." Once inside, you'll uncover a handful of undocumented movie trailers inside most of the subsections: Christopher Reeve's area houses a trailer to *Somewhere in Time* (1980); Kirstie Alley's bio contains a trailer to *For Richer or for Poorer* (1997); Michael Paré's filmography contains a trailer for *Streets of Fire* (1984); and director John Carpenter's section features a trailer for his masterpiece, *The Thing* (1982).

Walt Disney Treasures: Davy Crockett

Disney/Buena Vista Home Entertainment ★ Series Began 1954 ★ **Starring** Fess Parker, Buddy Ebsen

This limited edition (and numbered) Disney two-disc set features every episode of the 1954–55 *Davy Crockett* TV series, chronicling the adventures of the King of the Wild Frontier.

There's a well-hidden and rewarding Easter egg for fans of this classic black-and-white series. Insert disc 2, and from the main menu scroll down to select "Supplemental Features." Once inside, scroll down once to highlight the words "A Conversation with Fess Parker" but don't press Enter just yet. Instead, press the Right Arrow on the DVD remote and Davy's coonskin cap will become illuminated. Press Enter to see an entertaining behind-the-scenes clip with Fess Parker and co. singing "The Ballad of Davy Crockett."

Walt Disney Treasures: Mickey Mouse in Black and White

Disney/Buena Vista Home Entertainment ★ Series Began 1928

M-i-c-k-e-y, M-o-u-s-e. C'mon, you know the tune.

This collectible Disney two-disc set encased in a steel tin includes 34 original Mickey Mouse black-and-white cartoons and a limited edition collectible lithograph.

Naturally, there's a clever Easter egg, too. Pop in the first disc and from the main menu scroll down and select "Bonus Material." Once inside, scroll down to the bottom of the screen and highlight the words "Register Your DVD"—but don't press Enter just yet. Instead, tap the Up Arrow on the DVD remote and Mickey's cowboy hat will glow. Now press Enter to launch a clip featuring Leonard Maltin, who chats about the original Mickey Mouse clubs held in movie theaters in 1929, followed by the rare cartoon "Minnie's Yoo-Hoo."

Walt Disney Treasures: Mickey Mouse in Living Color

Disney/Buena Vista Home Entertainment ★ Series Began 1935

Mickey Mouse made his color debut during the dirty '30s—and this two-disc collectible DVD set immortalizes the classic cartoon series with 26 original episodes.

Want to know how to unlock the hidden eggs? OK, we'll tell you. On the first disc, highlight the words "Play All" from the main menu, but don't press Enter. Instead, tap the Right Arrow on the DVD remote and Mickey's head will illuminate in yellow. Now press Enter to see a clip of Walt Disney talking about the origin (and evolution) of the world's most famous mouse.

Now pop in the second disc and from the main menu once again scroll down and highlight the words "Play All" without pressing Enter just yet. Instead, press the Up Arrow and a pair of yellow Mickey Mouse ears will appear over the letter *o* in the word "Mouse." Now press Enter to enjoy the rare 1939 short film "Mickey's Surprise Party," prefaced by Leonard Maltin.

WarGames

MGM ★ Released 1983 ★ **Directed by** John Badham ★ **Starring** Matthew Broderick, Dabney Coleman, John Wood, Ally Sheedy

Teenager David Lightman (Matthew Broderick) is a talented computer user who accidentally hacks into the WOPR military computer, which may start World War III because it thinks it's playing a game.

The DVD for *WarGames* has a small but entertaining egg buried on it. From the main menu, tap the Left Arrow on the DVD remote and the tic-tac-toe game on the left-hand side of the screen will become illuminated. Now press Enter and you'll hear the classic "Shall we play a game?" as the computer, Joshua, plays itself into a frenzy before exploding into pieces.

Did You Know?

Actor Matthew Broderick was only 21 years young when he starred as the computer-savvy David Lightman in *WarGames*. This film also happened to be the one to launch his fruitful career. "Ferris Bueller, you're my hero."

Wayne's World

Paramount Pictures ★ **Released** 1992 ★ **Directed by** Penelope Spheeris ★
Starring Mike Myers, Dana Carvey, Rob Lowe

©2003 Paramount Home Entertainment.

Two goofy teenagers, Wayne (Mike Myers) and Garth (Dana Carvey), are approached by a sleazy TV exec (Rob Lowe) to bring their cable-access television show out of Wayne's basement.

The DVD features a few cute Easter egg gags—right on the main menu. Pop in the disc and you'll notice that there's a TV show listing at the bottom of the screen. Scroll down to the schedule and select "The Brady Bunch" on channel 12. You'll be treated to a funny scene from the '70s TV show, complete with a "Marsha, Marsha, Marsha!" line from Jan. Then do the same with "Solid Gold Workout" on Cable 10. Enjoy this clip from the TV show. Gotta love those '80s haircuts and workout clothes. Try it again with *Sunburn,* a 1979 movie staring Farrah Fawcett. It can be found on channel 11. What a steamy scene with Joan Collins!

What Lies Beneath

20th Century Fox/DreamWorks SKG ★ **Released** 2000 ★ **Directed by** Robert Zemeckis ★ **Starring** Harrison Ford, Michelle Pfeiffer

Courtesy of DreamWorks Home Entertainment.

In this supernatural thriller, Norman and Claire Spencer (Harrison Ford and Michelle Pfeiffer) are a seemingly happy married couple who begin to see frightening images in their home. But as in any good suspense story, there's a lot more that "lies beneath" the surface of their ghostly troubles.

Here's how to access the Easter eggs buried on this disc: Pop in the DVD and from the main menu press Stop twice. Now press "3" on the DVD remote (or "Search, 3" on some players) to start a 30-second DTS commercial as seen in some theaters. Crank up the speakers and get ready to be impressed!

If you have trouble starting this clip (as some DVD players may not allow manual chapter access too easily), use a computer's DVD software to access this egg.

The second egg is during the movie at the last scene. When the camera pans back after Michelle Pfeiffer's character walks out of the cemetery, look for a silhouette of a girl's face in the snow. Creepy!

Who Framed Roger Rabbit?

Touchstone Pictures ★ Released 1988 **★ Directed** by Robert Zemeckis ★ **Starring** Bob Hoskins, Christopher Lloyd

This Academy Award-winning film—which successfully fused live action with cartoon characters—is about a toon-hating detective (Bob Hoskins) who is Roger Rabbit's only hope in proving his innocence in the murder of Toontown's owner, Marvin Acme.

This two-DVD set is chock-full of bonus materials, plus there are some fun eggs to find, too, on both discs.

Insert the first DVD and don't press anything for a while. Benny the Cab will give you a hard time by screaming things like "So, where to, already?" "C'mon, my meter's running," "I ain't got all day!" and "We're going nowhere fast. Real fast!"

When you've had enough verbal abuse, move your cursor over the words "Movie Theatre" but don't press Enter. Instead, press the Down Arrow four times until the gauge on the car turns yellow. Now press Enter to see a hidden theatrical trailer for *Who Framed Roger Rabbit?*

For the second set of eggs on this disc, go back to the main menu and then select "Acme Warehouse." While here, move the cursor around and you'll see a few sets of cartoon eyes. Press Enter to watch animated gags on the screen, such as shoes walking around, fireworks exploding, and food thrown at the screen. In the middle set of boxes, press the Down Arrow and some green goo will appear on one of the boxes. Press Enter to unlock three bonus clips: "The Roger Rabbit Shorts," "Who Made Roger Rabbit?" and the "Trouble in Toontown" game. You can watch these or click the box on the bottom of the screen to go back to the Acme Warehouse. Now press the Down Arrow one more time and a chalk outline will appear on the floor. Press Enter and a giant safe will fall from the skies!

On the second DVD, select "Valiant Files," the third item down on the list. Move the cursor around Eddie's office and press Enter every time you see a green magnifying glass pop up. Pressing Enter on these will give you clues, including how to open the safe on the left-hand side of the screen. In case you don't find the crumpled piece of paper in the desk drawer, the correct combination is 40-60-10. A sweet surprise lies inside!

Willow

LucasFilm/20th Century Fox ★ Released 1988 **★ Directed by** Ron Howard **★ Starring** Val Kilmer, Joanne Whalley, Warwick Davis, Billy Barty, Jean Marsh

This two-hour fantasy adventure combines a compelling story, memorable characters, and dazzling special effects in an epic tale of good versus evil.

There's a special treat hidden on this disc for those savvy enough to find it. Here's the trick: From the main menu, select the last option, "Special Features." Once inside, enter the submenu entitled "TV Spots and Trailers." Now scroll down to the bottom of the screen and highlight the word "More"—but don't press Enter. Instead, press the Right Arrow on the DVD remote and a glowing fairy will appear out of nowhere. Now press Enter to view an eight-minute narrated featurette, "The Making of Raziel's Transformation." George Lucas is interviewed throughout this behind-the-scenes extra. Great stuff.

Wing Commander

20th Century Fox ★ Released 1999 **★ Directed by** Chris Roberts **★ Starring** Freddie Prinze Jr., Saffron Burrows, Matthew Lillard, Tcheky Karyo

Based on a space-combat computer game series of the same name, *Wing Commander* tells of a daring crew trying to sway the evil Kilrathi race from reaching—and destroying—planet Earth.

There's a small Easter egg on this disc, and it's pretty easy to access, too. From the main menu, press the Right Arrow on the DVD remote and the radar screen will become illuminated in red before you are launched into the hidden credits screen for this disc. B1 Media was responsible for the disc's custom menu interface, menu animation, and menu audio effects. Hey, give credit where credit is due!

The Wizard of Oz

Warner Bros. ★ **Released** 1939 ★ **Directed by** Victor Fleming ★ **Starring** Judy Garland, Ray Bolger, Jack Haley, Bert Lahr

Heralded as the best family film of all time by the American Film Institute, *The Wizard of Oz* tells the tale of the young Dorothy Gale (Judy Garland), who is swept away to a magical, song-filled adventure along the yellow brick road.

From the main menu of this feature-packed DVD, access the "Follow The Road To Oz" section to view a host of special features.

Select "Characters of Oz," and then scroll down and choose Glinda. Press the Up Arrow on the remote, and the yellow globe above her wand will illuminate in yellow. Press Enter to read some undocumented info on the Munchkins. Did you know these hardworking little people spent seven weeks filming at MGM and were paid from $35 to $75 a week (plus room and board)?

Also, on the "Wicked Witch of the West" character screen, press the Up Arrow and a yellow hourglass will appear. Press Enter to read secret facts about the Winged Monkeys.

In fact, if you tap the Left Arrow on many of these character pages, the ruby red slippers in the lower-left of the screen will illuminate, taking you to new hidden pages with additional information about the actors.

X-MEN

20th Century Fox ★ **Released** 2000 ★ **Directed by** Bryan Singer ★ **Starring** Patrick Stewart, Ian McKellen

In this popular comic book–turned Hollywood blockbuster, Professor Xavier (Patrick Stewart) helps a group of mutants come to grips with and harness their special powers. Together, they must foil the plot of the sinister Magneto (Ian McKellen), who believes humans and mutants cannot coexist.

The DVD for this sci-fi action flick features two Easter eggs.

The first can be accessed by going to the "Special Features" section and choosing

"Theatrical Trailers and TV Spots." Once here, press the Left Arrow, and a yellow rose will appear on the screen. Press Enter and sit back and enjoy a very funny joke played on the cast of the film involving an unexpected visitor.

The second surprise is in the "Art Gallery" area of the "Special Features" section. Press the Right Arrow twice, and Wolverine's dog tags will illuminate. Press Enter to read about two characters—"The Blob" and "The Beast"—who were cut from the film. Press the Right Arrow to scroll through six pages of preliminary sketches and drawings.

Young Guns: Special Edition

Artisan ★ Released 1988 ★ **Directed by** Christopher Cain ★ **Starring** Emilio Estevez, Kiefer Sutherland, Lou Diamond Phillips, Charlie Sheen, Dermot Mulroney, Casey Siemaszko

In 1878, six rebellious gunslingers—led by Billy the Kid (Emilio Estevez)—are hired to protect a British ranch owner's property against the ruthless Santa Fe Ring. But the boys become outlaws after war breaks out, spawning the largest manhunt in Western history.

There's a hidden Easter egg on this DVD, and here's how to find it: From the main menu, select "Special Features" from the list of available options. Now scroll down and highlight the words "Main Menu" but don't press Enter just yet. Instead, press the Right Arrow on the DVD remote and then the Up Arrow and the gun will turn blue (above the word "Credits"). Now press Enter to watch a "Young Guns" rap video, created specially for this "Special Edition DVD." Look, we didn't say this song was any *good*, but it's a hidden rap video nonetheless.

Did You Know?

Ben Stiller, who starred, co-wrote, directed, and produced Zoolander (page 183) also had his dad, Jerry Stiller, play the role of the slimy "Maury Ballstein." A veteran actor and comedian, Jerry Stiller is best known with today's generation as Frank Costanza from *Seinfeld* (1993–1998), George's neurotic father. His first TV series, however, was 1948's *Toast of the Town*.

You've Got Mail

Warner Bros. Pictures ★ Released 1998 **★ Directed by** Nora Ephron ★
Starring Tom Hanks, Meg Ryan, Parker Posey, Jean Stapleton, Dave Chappelle, Steve Zahn, Dabney Coleman, Greg Kinnear

From director Nora Ephron (*Sleepless in Seattle*, *When Harry Met Sally*, *Michael*) comes this heartwarming romantic comedy about two people who fall for one another in cyberspace—but then find out they're business rivals.

There are a couple of Easter eggs hidden on this disc. From the main menu, click over to the "Special Features" section and then click on "The Mail Room." Once inside, click to start watching the HBO documentary entitled "HBO First Look Special: A Conversation with Nora Ephron."

Using your "Skip Forward" button on the DVD remote (it looks something like this: >>|), press once to go to the next chapter on the disc. Here you'll find comparisons of key scenes from *You've Got Mail* to older films the film is loosely based on: *The Shop Around the Corner* (1940) and *In the Good Old Summertime* (1949).

These extras can also be accessed using a DVD-ROM drive and supported software.

Wait, there's more! There are also four undocumented interview clips to watch— select Chapter 1, Titles 57, 58, 59, and 60.

Zoolander

Paramount Pictures ★ Released 2001 **★ Directed by** Ben Stiller **★ Starring** Ben Stiller, Owen Wilson

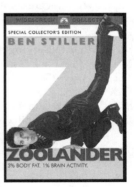

High fashion meets hilarious comedy in this story about a clueless model, Derek Zoolander (Ben Stiller), who is brainwashed into killing the Prime Minister of Malaysia.

Zoolander contains a little-known—and quite humorous—video clip with commentary.

From the disc's main menu, click on the "Special Features" menu, and then select "More" to get to the second page. Now click on "Photo Galleries," and press the Right Arrow to highlight the spinning *M* symbol on the screen.

Press Enter to watch a rehearsal tape featuring Zoolander (Stiller) and Hansel (Owen Wilson) practicing their climactic "walk-off" catwalk sequence.

INTERNATIONAL CONTACT INFORMATION

AUSTRALIA
McGraw-Hill Book Company
Australia Pty. Ltd.
TEL +61-2-9900-1800
FAX +61-2-9878-8881
http://www.mcgraw-hill.com.au
books-it_sydney@mcgraw-hill.com

CANADA
McGraw-Hill Ryerson Ltd.
TEL +905-430-5000
FAX +905-430-5020
http://www.mcgraw-hill.ca

GREECE, MIDDLE EAST, & AFRICA
(Excluding South Africa)
McGraw-Hill Hellas
TEL +30-210-6560-990
TEL +30-210-6560-993
TEL +30-210-6560-994
FAX +30-210-6545-525

MEXICO (Also serving Latin America)
McGraw-Hill Interamericana Editores
S.A. de C.V.
TEL +525-1500-5108
FAX +525-117-1589
http://www.mcgraw-hill.com.mx
carlos_ruiz@mcgraw-hill.com

SINGAPORE (Serving Asia)
McGraw-Hill Book Company
TEL +65-6863-1580
FAX +65-6862-3354
http://www.mcgraw-hill.com.sg
mghasia@mcgraw-hill.com

SOUTH AFRICA
McGraw-Hill South Africa
TEL +27-11-622-7512
FAX +27-11-622-9045
robyn_swanepoel@mcgraw-hill.com

SPAIN
McGraw-Hill/
Interamericana de España, S.A.U.
TEL +34-91-180-3000
FAX +34-91-372-8513
http://www.mcgraw-hill.es
professional@mcgraw-hill.es

UNITED KINGDOM, NORTHERN, EASTERN, & CENTRAL EUROPE
McGraw-Hill Education Europe
TEL +44-1-628-502500
FAX +44-1-628-770224
http://www.mcgraw-hill.co.uk
emea_queries@mcgraw-hill.com

ALL OTHER INQUIRIES Contact:
McGraw-Hill/Osborne
TEL +1-510-420-7700
FAX +1-510-420-7703
http://www.osborne.com
omg_international@mcgraw-hill.com

Sound Off!

Visit us at **www.osborne.com/bookregistration** and let us know what you thought of this book. While you're online you'll have the opportunity to register for newsletters and special offers from McGraw-Hill/Osborne.

We want to hear from you!

Sneak Peek

Visit us today at **www.betabooks.com** and see what's coming from McGraw-Hill/Osborne tomorrow!

Based on the successful software paradigm, Bet@Books™ allows computing professionals to view partial and sometimes complete text versions of selected titles online. Bet@Books™ viewing is free, invites comments and feedback, and allows you to "test drive" books in progress on the subjects that interest you the most.